# ORDER

from

# CHAOS

# ORDER
## from
# CHAOS

A Six-Step Plan for
Organizing Yourself,
Your Office, and
Your Life

# LIZ DAVENPORT

 THREE RIVERS PRESS
NEW YORK

Published by Three Rivers Press, New York, New York.
Member of the Crown Publishing Group.

Random House, Inc. New York, Toronto, London, Sydney, Auckland
www.randomhouse.com

THREE RIVERS PRESS and the Tugboat design are registered trademarks of Random House, Inc.

Printed in the United States of America

Design by Helene Berinsky

Library of Congress Cataloging-in-Publication Data

Davenport, Liz.
   Order from chaos: a six-step plan for organizing yourself, your office, and your life / by Liz Davenport.
      1. Time management. 2. Self-management (Psychology) 3. Office management. I. Title.

HD69.T54 D375 2001
650.1—dc21                          2001027759

ISBN 0-609-80777-3

10 9 8 7 6 5 4 3 2 1

First Edition

To Bob
for all his patience, support, and love
with this "creative genius magpie"
Thank you, Sweetie!

# CONTENTS

## I'M DONE . . . SO NOW WHAT?

# BEFORE
# YOU BEGIN . . .

# Why Get Organized?

The average businessperson receives 190 pieces of information *each day*. The average businessperson wastes 150 hours *each year* looking for stuff. Add 10 more hours and that is an entire work month. If you got organized, you could have an extra month each year! Just think how much more you could accomplish (or how much vacation you could have) if you got organized. You could take a three-day weekend every other week and still do as much as you are doing now—or MORE. What a concept.

Most of us have some sort of organizing system or, more likely, multiple systems. Unfortunately, those systems are not all-encompassing. They have holes, things that don't fit or aren't accounted for within the system you have designed. The piles on your desk result from holes in your system (as well as from the incoming 190 pieces of information each day). What you need is one, all-encompassing organizing system. Until you have one, simple, intuitive, easy-to-maintain system, attempting to clean off your desk will only thwart, exhaust, and annoy you. And your desk won't stay clean for long.

The average businessperson receives 190 pieces of information each day . . .
and wastes 150 hours each year just looking for stuff.

One of the major benefits of having a single, comprehensive system is that we don't have to make thousands of little decisions each day, such as "What do I do with *this* piece of paper?" "Where can I put this so I can find it again later when I need it?" Making 190 of those decisions each day is emotionally and mentally exhausting. Once you have a system, you *know* where those pieces of paper go, and it is simply a matter of putting them there.

You also need to change the way you think about those 190 pieces of new, incoming information each day. The biggest mistake disorganized folks make is believing there is a "later." For us, there is only "now" and "too late." All the things we optimistically put off till later end up just lying there for days, weeks, months, or years. How old are some of the things in your stacks? We need to develop methods for making decisions about things as they come in, not waiting till that magical hour in the mythical "later" miraculously appears. Then and only then can you begin get control of your own personal chaos.

What qualifies me to help those of you who are by nature disorganized? Because I am just like you. *I* am, by nature, disorganized. I have the same personality profile as most of my clients; that is, we are creative, we hate details, we are spontaneous, and we like to leave things open-ended. We are the creative geniuses of the world. Our energy is focused on the future—the next project, the next idea, the next grand scheme. Unfortunately, paper belongs to the past or, at best, the present. Our attention is on the future. Therefore, clutter is the natural side effect of being creative. That doesn't mean we don't have to deal with it; it just means we have a good excuse for our mess!

> Those of us who are disorganized are the creative geniuses of the world. Our energy is focused on the future ... paper belongs to the past.

Given my personality profile, I have just described someone you would probably *not* hire to help you get organized. Another factor comes into play; I was born legally blind. This problem went uncorrected until I was 30. The effect has been that since birth, if I did not *know* where something was, I couldn't find it by just looking for it. So I learned to create simple, disorganized-person-type systems that are easy to set up and maintain.

If you only have the energy to implement one thing from this book, make it Step 1, the Cockpit Office. If you have the inclination to go further, implement Step 2, Air Traffic Control. Do not do Step 3 only, or Step 6 only, because each step builds on the last. I recommend spending at least one week accomplishing each step, but I don't care how long it takes you to do all the steps, just do them in order, please. What is offered here is a very simple system for businesspeople. It works for everyone, even you, because of its *simplicity*. You can modify it to fit your individual circumstances, but the basics apply to anybody who has a desk. So get going and get organized!

# The Game Plan

Some of us need to have the big picture before we are willing to listen to the details, so here is an overview of the whole system. Each step is intended to be executed over the course of a week. At the end of each chapter is a detailed checklist.

## ABOUT THESE GRAY BOXES . . .

If you are one of those folks who wants "just the facts," you can skip the gray boxes within the text. They are the stories, illustrations, and/or personal examples included for those of us who need more of a "why" to go with our "what to do."

One tip for success . . . getting organized is *not* a solitary activity. You will more likely succeed if you have someone to discuss things with, work with, or just to help keep you on track. Otherwise, you may easily get sidetracked, find something else to do, or simply never quite get around to it. So tackle this project with a friend, a family member, or a coworker. Share your schedule with them for the entire six-week program and ask them to ask you for weekly updates.

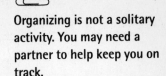

**Organizing is not a solitary activity. You may need a partner to help keep you on track.**

If you still have trouble getting off the dime, then invite them over for no more than four hours at a time. Fix them a pot of coffee (or a pitcher of margaritas) and tell them their job is not to touch anything, but rather to keep you on task. It is far easier for them to toss stuff—it isn't their stuff and they are not attached to it like you are. Truth be told, it will proba-bly *all* look like junk to them. Keep to a schedule. Allow no more than 30 seconds for keep/toss decisions. Five seconds is even better. In your heart of hearts you know immediately what to do with your old stuff, you just let your fear get in the way.

### STEP 1: THE COCKPIT OFFICE

When you sit down at your desk to work you should have everything you need to complete any project. Many of us believe that having other people interrupt us is the biggest waste of our time. In reality, interrupting ourselves is the real thief of our time.

Consider your desk your "Cockpit." Inside your Cockpit you want only "now," "happening" kinds of things, not old, archaic, moldy things that have not seen the light of day in years. For example, consider that file drawer in your desk, the one easiest to reach. What's in it? I'll bet you cannot even

## THE SIX STEPS

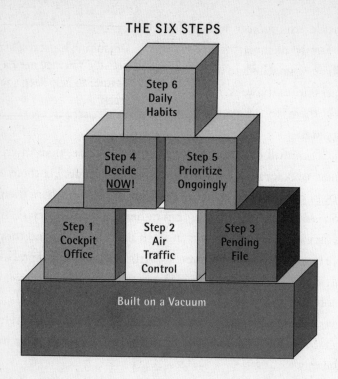

name, much less use, some of the things in it. It is a place where things go in and never come out again. They are often "important" things, not frequently used things. If the drawer contains some frequently used things, they are probably only in the front couple of inches. Sound familiar? Step 1, then, is to create the Cockpit Office, a space where you have only the *essential* tools necessary to do your work.

### STEP 2: AIR TRAFFIC CONTROL

If you need to remember to do something, how do you remember to do it? You probably put that important piece of paper on the desk in front of you where you can see it. The next important thing you absolutely must not forget to do goes in front of you, too. The next follows suit, and on and on, ad infinitum. Soon

**This book is designed to be implemented one step each week in order. Don't try to do Step 2 until you have completed Step 1, and so on.**

you are buried under important pieces of paper, and every time you look at them, you ask yourself, "I wonder what is in that pile that I am forgetting to do?" Up goes your stress level. Creating an Air Traffic Control system is the alternative to the "out of sight, out of mind" methodology that most folks use. Your Air Traffic Controller is your single radar screen for each day and contains

- a section for appointments,
- a section for to-do's, and
- a section for important notes relevant to that day.

So far, the greatest number of calendars any one of my clients was using concurrently was eight. How many do you use? If you have one you carry with you to write appointments on, one on your computer, one on the front of the refrigerator the family uses, and one on the desk pad at the office, how can you possibly expect to not miss something sometime? We are not even going to talk about the sticky notes everywhere or about all those things you carry around in your head. It is too much for anyone to check all of them every time. You need *one* system, one radar screen that allows you to schedule activities for *one day at a time*, so you only have to look at them when you *need to act on them*. You do not need to have them lying around cluttering up your desk and making you feel overwhelmed.

The notes page in your Air Traffic Controller (to be explained in detail later) replaces the 17 layers of sticky notes, the backs of envelopes, and the odd scraps with pertinent data on them as well as the reports, agendas, meeting notices, and copies of things already lost at least once, which many of us typically have lying around on our desks so we will "have them when we need them."

## STEP 3: THE PENDING FILE

Many clients think the Pending File is the best idea I offer them. The Pending File works hand in hand with Air Traffic Control to get rid of clutter. When you find a piece of paper that requires action later, but does not need its own individual file folder, you note the required action on the appropriate day in your Air Traffic Controller. Then you put the supporting piece of paper in the Pending File. There it is, out of the way but *not* forgotten. Simple yet brilliant, yes?

At this point, we will have mastered the physical environment. It is time to deal with "every piece of paper" in your life. To more fully refine and personalize your office, we need to look at what other systems, routines, and repetitive tasks we can systematize to streamline the workday. After Step 3 is completed, you will have one, simple, all-encompassing system for all the papers, appointments, and to-do's in your life.

Now we go to level two, where we deal with your *attitudes* about those 190 bits of information that come in each day.

### STEP 4: MAKE DECISIONS

How many things can you do in a day? 10? 20? 50? If 190 requests are made of you each day and you can only do 20, how many times do you need to say "No"? Do you say "No" 170 times each day, or do you say "Maybe" or "Later" or "I'd like to someday"? Much of the clutter surrounding you is simply generated by those unmade decisions.

> Do you say "No," or do you say "Maybe" or "Later" or "I'd like to someday?" Much of the clutter surrounding you is simply generated by unmade decisions.

How many times do you pick up a piece of paper, look at it, say "I don't know what to do with this," and set it back down? The first time you have a piece of paper in your hand, you know 99.9 percent of the time as much as you will ever know about that piece of paper. So JUST MAKE A DECISION. When we do not have a system, the process of deciding what to do with each piece of paper is exhausting. Once we have a system, it is a snap.

When I work with clients and they say, "I don't know what to do with this," I ask "What is it?" "Why are you saving it?" "What action is required?" and "Should you really just throw it away?" Somewhere in the series of questions, they tell me what should be done with the paper. Then I point out that they really *did know* what to do with the paper, they just *weren't doing it*. Why? We, as human beings, have an addiction to paper. We save paper we do not need. Therefore, the plan is make a decision the first time you have it in your hand; shorten the process and eliminate the clutter.

### STEP 5: PRIORITIZE ONGOINGLY

(I realize I "Ogden-Nashed" a word here, but our language doesn't have one quite as perfect.) Most of us are being "nibbled to death by ducks." By that I mean, we are each inundated with niggling little things each day that eat up our time. "Ducks" are those unnecessary, unproductive phone calls that interrupt us on our landlines, cell phones, pagers, satellite dishes. They are the other people's emergencies we get sucked into, as well as the faxes and e-mails, which assume a status of urgency by their very nature regardless of their true status, and on and on. Statistics have shown that only 15 percent of daily interruptions are truly worth your attention. That means 85 percent of them are wasting your time. Meanwhile, the truly important things we need to accomplish fall by the wayside. Prioritizing helps us to focus on the essential stuff and avoid the "ducks."

> Statistics have shown that only 15 percent of daily interruptions are truly worth your attention. That means 85 percent of them are wasting your time. Meanwhile, the essential things we need to accomplish fall by the wayside.

First, prioritize your Air Traffic Control daily radar screen. Remember Step 2? (This also helps sidestep procrastination, by the way, but more on that later.) Then, weigh the incoming "ducks" against your progress on the already identified most important tasks on your list. If you don't write down what you need to do, and prioritize that list, you have nothing to measure the "ducks" against. Last, but certainly not least, is Step 6.

## STEP 6: PLAN YOUR DAY, END YOUR DAY, CLEAN OFF YOUR DESK AT THE END OF THE DAY

Once you have conquered your physical environment and modified your attitude about the incoming, you are now ready to institute some daily habits.

Plan Your Day means to start your day by reviewing your radar screen (your appointments and to-do's) and prioritizing your day. It includes having at least one item that is a baby step toward a larger goal on your list. Once you have created a plan, you have obtained the assistance of your greatest ally, your subconscious, to help you in manifesting your plan.

> Once you have created a plan, you have obtained the assistance of your greatest ally, your subconscious, to help you in manifesting your plan.

You can focus your energy where it will be most effective and enter your day head-on, calm, prepared, and in control.

End Your Day means to review your radar screen, check off the tasks that are completed, reschedule any tasks that are still incomplete, and have closure with your day—finished, complete. This component is absolutely necessary for those of us who have brains that won't shut off. It can be

> Ending the day is absolutely necessary for those of us who have brains that won't shut off.

the greatest gift to not wake up at 3 A.M. with an "Oh NO! I forgot to ____ (fill in the blank)." This is an amazing way to improve your sleep patterns.

Clean Off Your Desk at the End of the Day means just that. Once you have conquered your physical environment and are making decisions as things come in and prioritizing ongoingly, cleaning off the desk at the end of eight or so hours should be a cakewalk. I mean, really, how much can accumulate in eight hours? Certainly you will have a different answer than if you only are cleaning off your desk weekly, monthly, or yearly—as you may be doing now, eh?

So, that is it . . . what do you think? Doable? You bet, so let's start and . . .

**GO GET ORGANIZED!**

# THE
# PHYSICAL
# ENVIRONMENT

# Preorganizing—
# Creating a Vacuum

OVERWHELMING AMOUNTS OF OLD STUFF ALERT!

READ THIS ALERT FIRST!

It contains vital motivational information.

If you *do not* have tons, piles, and scads of old stuff to deal with, skip this chapter for now and go straight to "Step 1: The Cockpit Office."

If you *do* have tons, piles, and scads of old stuff, start with "Preorganizing—Creating a Vacuum."

But *do not* let dealing with the old stuff cause you to lose momentum and quit. If the old stuff is too daunting, just put it in boxes and stuff it away somewhere out of sight. Later, when you have had some wins, come back to it with renewed vigor.

## Creating a Vacuum

What is a vacuum? A vacuum is the empty space in drawers, bookcases, filing cabinets, and closets in which to put all the new stuff that is coming in each day. Each file drawer should have at least two inches of play in it so when you want to file something, you can easily open the file with two fingers and drop in whatever you need to file. When files are too jam-packed to easily file in, most people quit filing! It's true! That is when we start setting things on top of the file cabinet saying "I'll file that later . . ." and, of course, later never comes. The next time we have something to file in that same cabinet, we see the existing pile, add the new to the old, and say again "I'll file it all later" and so on.

**This old stuff takes up physical space, but it also takes up psychological space; if your office is full of old, useless stuff, so is your head.**

You need a vacuum in your office for two reasons. First, it *must* be easier to be organized than it is to be disorganized, or we won't do it. Second, most of us never clear out files, closets, and bookcases of the *old* stuff, the stuff we are no longer using and may never use again. This old stuff takes up physical space, but *it also takes up psychological space*; if your office is full of old, useless stuff, so is your head.

What old baggage do you have and why? Everything you keep should be something that lifts you up, makes you feel happier and lighter (old tax documents are, of course, the exception). If you do not have a vacuum, why not? What are you hoarding that you need to let go of, both physically and mentally?

## CASE STUDY

I have a client who had 35 boxes in her garage that she had carried with her for more than 15 years in numerous moves across four different states. She had never actually *opened* the boxes or *looked* into them or retrieved anything *out of* them, but she was absolutely convinced it was all priceless and not one item contained therein could be thrown away. Finally, her husband, who was tired of tripping over her boxes, made her an offer. He promised to buy her a new car, *any* new car of her choice, with the stipulation that she had to be able to park it on *her* side of the garage (just where the 35 boxes were living). As you can imagine, I received a frantic phone call. "We just HAVE to get rid of those boxes, Liz darling, but HOW?"

We started bright and early one morning. We opened the first box and my client said "Oh, look! This is from a job I had 15 years ago." In the box was a brochure she had created at that job—not just one copy, but more like 500 copies. We agreed keeping one was sufficient and put the other 499 in the recycling bin. Next was a press release she had written at the same job. She had not only the final published press release, but also the 17 previous drafts of the same press release. We agreed the final was sufficient, and the other 17 previous versions could go. And on it went, all day. By the time we were done the story had emerged. These boxes were from a job she had gotten laid off from 15 years ago. What she had boxed up was not paper—it was her self-esteem. She had amassed everything she had ever done in that job so she had *proof* of how good she was and how wrong they were to lay her off. No matter that she has never looked in any of those boxes ever again. Psychologically, she did not need to. Her subconscious knew what was in them and why. Eventually, we reduced 35 boxes to 2 boxes, which fit on a shelf at the back of the garage, and she got her new car!

One would expect that the story ends there, but two months later her accountant called her and said, "What in the heck did you do?" "What do you mean?" she asked. Her accountant said, "The net income for your business has gone up by 25 percent in the last two months. What did you do?" What she had done was to let go of the old baggage. Not just the physical baggage of 35 boxes, but also the psychological baggage of the anger, the fear, the rejection. When she let go of the old, both physically and mentally, she made room for the new: new clients, new ideas, new confidence, and enthusiasm.

How do you create this vacuum? First, let's discuss the Vacuum Creating Rules. These rules apply to the entire process, no matter where you are working.

### RULE #1: DON'T GET BOGGED DOWN

The biggest caveat for the beginner with tons of baggage is, don't get bogged down in creating a vacuum if it will stop you from moving on to the next steps. Just put all the really old stuff in boxes and put it behind you or in a closet or a garage—just somewhere where you cannot see it for now. Don't worry about what is in there, especially if it is old. If you don't know that you have it or you can't find it—YOU DON'T REALLY HAVE IT now, do you? It is far more important that you learn to deal with the 190 new pieces of information that are coming at you each day. If you are not dealing with that each day, you are only going to be creating more backlog (read baggage). Let the old stuff sit, then deal with it a little at a time but only after you have dealt with the new. Make sense? Think about how long it took you to create that backlog. How could you possibly expect to clean it up in a day? So keep your focus on the new. The old will wait for you.

## RULE #2: GET THESE SUPPLIES

You will need containers for your stuff. The temporary containers can be cardboard, as they will be going away soon. The containers for things to be stored are another matter. If the area where things will be stored is climatically controlled (like in your office closet or a closet in the building), cardboard boxes with lids will work. In office supply stores these are frequently referred to as "banker's boxes" and require assembly by you. The generic ones hold file folders but *not* hanging folders. Some are specially designed to hold hanging folders and are slightly more expensive. If the area is *not* climatically controlled (like a garage or storage area), plastic boxes with lids may be a better choice. Some folks simply prefer plastic because things that are hermetically sealed are protected from dust, humidity, vermin, and so on. Plastic is usually more expensive, but not significantly so. Plastic boxes are also stronger if the boxes will need to be stored on top of each other rather than on shelves. The choice is yours.

### RULE #3: CREATE THESE BOXES

You will need two boxes where you can put things that will require action by you. Since this is old stuff, you should not be finding anything you urgently need to take action on (otherwise somebody would have already bugged you about it or sent you another notice on it). Most of the material will be things you saved because you thought it would be nice to do someday. Label one box **To-Do Now** and label another box **To-Do Later.** Don't be too optimistic about how much you can do. Keep in mind the 190 new items each day.

The other category you will most likely find things belong in is **Archive.** Archival stuff includes things you don't use very often (less than once a month) but that need to be kept

---

#### OPTIMISM GONE WRONG

Overly optimistic behavior about how much you can accomplish creates "too much to do" and "I'll get around to it later" problems in other areas as well. Having too many unfinished projects is actually a common problem in our homes, too. For example, when you are dusting, you knock over the little shepherdess figurine and her hand breaks off. What do you do with it? You set it on the kitchen counter and say to yourself, "I'll glue that in just a minute," and you truly believe that as soon as you are done cleaning the house, you will glue her hand. But, when you are done cleaning, something else catches your attention or your time and you don't get around to her. So there she sits two days, two weeks, two months later. Every time you pass her, she calls to you "glue me," as does every other similar project in the house. You are bombarded by drapes crying "hem me," pictures calling "hang me up," ceiling fans screaming "dust me," and umpteen other household items with their own little voices. No wonder we are frazzled.

This is an example of how overwhelmed and jam-packed our lives have become. There is a way to shut up all those little voices. Walk around the house with a clipboard and write down *everything* you see that is crying out to you. Next, prioritize that list. Say to yourself "If I only get one thing on this list done, what should it be?" and put a 1 next to that. Then ask "If I only get two things done, what should the second one be?" and put a 2 next to that one. Now, take the top five or ten and schedule them on your calendar. Don't put them all on one day. Pepper them throughout a month or so. Finally, put the figurines and pictures in a closet until their number comes up. As for the ceiling fans and the drapes, when they holler to you, tell them "You are on the list, so shut up!"

for future use. To archive your old stuff does not mean just tossing it willy-nilly in boxes and hiding it away. Your archived stuff needs to be organized so you can find individual items again, if you need them. So how do you create this archive?

## RULE #4: CLEARLY LABEL WHAT YOU ARCHIVE

If you use cardboard boxes with lids, write on the outside with a waterproof, thick, dark marker. If you use plastic, you may need to attach a paper to the outside to make notes on. Whatever the box is made of, be sure to label the general contents clearly, in big letters you can see from a distance. Then in smaller print, note in detail what is inside each box. If you end up with 20 boxes lining your garage or closet, they must be clearly labeled so that if you *do* need to retrieve any of the things in them, you will know *exactly* which box to look in.

> Clearly label things you are keeping. The only thing worse than tons of old stuff is tons of old stuff in unlabeled boxes.

## RULE #5: GROUP LIKE OBJECTS

Things we save need to be grouped together with their friends. For example, have one clearly labeled box for all your old tax papers. If it takes more than one box, label each box with the years it contains.

Do not, I repeat, DO NOT spend much time at all organizing and categorizing old tax records and receipts. The only time you will need them is if you get audited. No matter how organized your receipts, if you get audited, you will be going over them again and again, anyway. So just have them so you can find them if needed. If you never get audited, you never need them again.

Have one clearly labeled box for memorabilia. Memorabilia is anything that has no intrinsic value, but you want to keep for sentimental reasons. This includes old photos, newspaper clippings, cards, things like that. Perhaps you have things from previous jobs. Then you might want to have one clearly labeled box for each old job. You can create categories in advance and/or as you come across them, as you recognize them. Do not create too many little bitty categories. The criterion is to have at least one box full of stuff in that category to qualify for its own box. If there will be less than an entire box, group one or more categories in a box, but do not split groups. If the choice is splitting a group or having a partially filled box, go with a partially filled box. You will probably have items to add later.

## RULE #6: THROW AWAY 95 PERCENT OF THE OLD STUFF

A little known fact is that 95 *percent* of everything you have saved for over six months is *trash*. The exception to this rule is tax papers, legal documents, and anything you are required by law to keep (people involved in the securities business know what I mean). The mistake most people make is in looking for the 5 percent to save, rather than looking for the 95 percent to trash. If you look for the 5 percent to save you will end up saving way more than 5 percent. Therefore, look for the 95 percent to throw away and you will have better luck.

> A little known fact is that *95 percent* of everything you have saved for over six months is *trash*.

Don't use the pick-and-choose method. Rather, take everything out, then put back what you are keeping. For example, file drawers. Don't just open the drawer, root around in it for what you need to get rid of, and close the drawer. Rather, take every file out of the drawer, decide the category the drawer will be when you are done (like clients, or personnel, or organizations), then put things back in as needed for that category and toss or archive whatever is left when you are done.

Enough theory, let's get started. Keeping the rules in mind, here is the step-by-step method.

## Start at the End, Not the Beginning

If you have a lot of really old stuff in your office, the worst thing you can do is to start with the top of your desk. If every drawer, every shelf, and every flat surface is already full, there is no place to put what comes off the top of your desk. You will eventually get frustrated and scream "This is hopeless!" So, *don't* start with the newest stuff, start with the *oldest* and work backwards until the top of your desk is the *last* place you clean.

> If you have a lot of piles of really *old* stuff in your office, the worst thing you can do is to start trying to clean up with the *top of your desk.*

To create your vacuum, therefore, you are going to go to the final repository of your oldest stuff and work backwards to the top of your desk. If your office closet is the final place, then start there. Be sure to include every closet, piece of furniture, and hidey-hole in your office. Go through the following list of locations, find the first one that applies to you, and start there.

## 1. CLOSET(s)

Take everything out, identifying the large categories as you go. For example you may find:

- extra office supplies
- three-ring notebooks
- old client/project files
- memorabilia
- letterhead and envelopes with an old logo
- old, out-of-date brochures
- old equipment that no longer works or is out of date
- holiday decorations

Identify the appropriate categories as you go, labeling boxes for permanent storage where appropriate, or labeling temporary boxes if the contents will be arranged differently. For example, permanently keeping extra office supplies in a cardboard box may be inconvenient; arranging them on a shelf at shoulder height may be better. Label a box with a sticky note "office supplies" to contain them until you are refilling the closet and it is time to arrange them.

Place things in the appropriate box (like "Memorabilia" or "Client Files '92–'96" or perhaps "Clients, Old—A through G"). The out-of-date brochures and letterhead with the old logo can go into the recycling bin if appropriate or the trash. You may keep one sample of each and put it in the "Memorabilia" box if you like, but get rid of the rest. You won't use them and they are taking up precious space. Old equipment can be fixed, if cost-effective, donated if at all useful, or simply tossed if necessary. Whatever you do with it, don't just put it back in the closet again. If you need to get permission to get rid of it, write a note to ask the boss and put it in the To-Do Now box. The holiday decorations can be clearly labeled, then put back in the closet, assuming they are something you actually use, but put them in the least accessible spot, like on the top shelf or on the floor in the back. They are the least frequently used item. Sort the office supplies, grouping like items. Then arrange them on an accessible shelf in groups; pens in one container, pencils in another, same size Post-it notes stacked together. Now you can find what you need when you need it. Only keep as many of an item as you will reasonably use. If you use five 8.5″ × 11″ mailing envelopes a month and you have been saving every one you have ever gotten until you are overrun, limiting the amount you keep would be wise. If you kept 30, that would be approximately a six-month supply, assuming normal usage. Define "enough" of any one item and store only that amount.

Do not be afraid of empty space. If you have shelves in the closet that are empty, good for you! You will continue to have things that will need to go into the closet, and if every square inch is already jam-packed, the new stuff will have nowhere to go. So space is good! Space is our friend!

### 2. BOOKCASE(s)

Empty the bookshelf, again identifying categories as you go. Appropriate categories may be computer manuals, business books, reference books, or organizational directories. If you have old computer manuals (for old versions of current software or software you no longer use) toss/recycle them. Toss previous years' organizational and phone directories. Keep only the current ones. Business books or reference books should be ones you have used at least once in the past year. Many of us have old college books we have not opened since the final, but we display them proudly like trophies. If you have not opened a book in the past year, archive, recycle, or toss it, whichever is most appropriate. Try to have one category per shelf. Be sure to leave plenty of room (at least six inches) on each shelf for expansion. If need be, label the shelf with its category until you get used to it, or if many folks use the same books.

### 3. FILING CABINET(s)

If you have a filing system where you can find things, then fine. Don't change it. If, on the other hand, your filing system is not the greatest, consider the following modifications. Many folks set up an A to Z filing system simply because they believe that is how it is done. The danger to an A to Z system is that you must remember exactly what you titled a file, or finding it again can be a nightmare. Those of us who are disorganized tend to make files with far too specific titles, believing that if we give a file a very specific title, we will be able to find it again. In reality we have *decreased* the odds that we will find it again. First we have to remember exactly what we called it. If I have filed my receipts, what did I call that file? Was it "Business Expenses," "Expense Reports," "Business Receipts," or "Expense Receipts"? That is a lot of places to look, especially if I was in a particularly analytical frame of mind the day I created the file and called it "Receipts, Business."

**CREATE DRAWER CATEGORIES** A better method for filing is to first create subcategories, rather than just A to Z. What are the four primary categories of the files in your file cabinet? Your categories may be Clients, Projects, Reference Materials, Organizations, Personnel, Training, Policies, Administration, Publications, Contracts, or Applications. And, *no*, you cannot use "Misc." or "Stuff" or "Etc." as titles! Once you decide on the categories, identify which drawer will contain each category. Arrange the drawers based on frequency of use. If you seldom use "Administration," put it in the bottom drawer. If you use "Clients" daily, make that the easiest to reach drawer. Once you have identified what each drawer will hold, LABEL IT ON THE OUTSIDE! Anybody else who has to find something in your files will thank you. Labeling the drawers will also keep you honest. You will be less likely to just stuff something in a drawer to get it out of sight.

**CREATE LARGER CATEGORIES WITHIN EACH DRAWER** Next, create larger categories within the subcategory. Administration may contain "Presentations" or "Monthly Reports" or "Policies & Procedures." The rule of thumb is, if a file will not *at some point in time* have at least 20 pieces of paper in it, the title is too specific. Let's take, for example, my filing method for car-related documents. In my file drawer called "Household" I have a file called "Car Stuff." Into it goes insurance, repairs, title, registration, anything having to do with any cars I own. Then, I always file chronologically in the front because of yet another little known fact. If you go looking in your files for something, you have a 90 percent chance it will be something you filed recently. That means 90 percent of the time what you are looking for will be one of the first three or four pieces of paper in the file. That is really quick! And it simplifies the process of filing it in the first place.

DON'T ASK "HOW SHOULD I FILE THIS?" BUT RATHER "HOW WILL I USE THIS?" Another rule for filing is to file things not where you think they should be filed, but rather according to how you will use them. The receipts from bills we pay will illustrate what I mean. Most folks have the files for their bills set up with a separate file for each bill. For example, there is one file for the phone bill, one for the gas, one for the water, one for their Visa, and so on. Now, as if it were not painful enough to have to pay the silly things, now you will have to spend another 15 to 30 minutes standing there filing the receipts in each individual file, assuming they even make it to files. A filing system that is time-consuming to use is frequently not used. The bills end up on top of the filing cabinet with you saying to yourself, "I'll file those tomorrow."

Here is a much simpler, faster method. Label 12 files "January," "February," "March," and so on; when you are done paying the bills, you simply open the appropriate month file, drop the bills in, and you are done! Much greater odds that you will do that, isn't there? If you need to refer to an old receipt, isn't it usually one that was paid just last month? In reality we need our cancelled check more than we need the actual bill. The bill only proves you were billed. The cancelled check proves you paid it!

Make it one step simpler, and just have a box where you throw the bills you've just paid on the top. If you are careful to maintain the order of the stack when you go back to look for something, this system is even easier. Remember, the definition of organized just means you can find it again.

Color can be used as well to assist in identification. Clients could be red; Organizations, yellow; General Administration, blue; Projects, white; or Finances, green. To save money and time (and not have to go out and buy billions of new file folders), you can use colored highlighters and simply highlight the existing file labels with the appropriate color. New files could be created in the appropriate color, but to try to go back and redo every file would be too much. Color makes it easier to get files back in the right drawer or avoid misfiling in the first place. If every file in a given drawer is red and the file you are about to put in there is yellow, it is pretty obvious something is wrong. When, for example, a client file is needed, you know exactly which drawer it is in, and do not have to wonder if it was filed under the company name, the representative's name, the owner's name, or the product name. It will be in the client drawer and eventually you can find it. When a file is lying on the desk, the color immediately identifies it as a specific category.

During the process of cleaning out the filing cabinet, do not be surprised at the amount of trash that is generated. Trash is a good thing! Also, keep an eye out for that which can be archived. Archived material will go in the existing archive boxes in the closet or new archive boxes created to go into the closet.

**COMPUTER FILES** Computer files should be handled in the same way as paper systems. Whoever came up with the idea of creating an area on the computer called "My Documents" was a sadist. I can't begin to count the number of innocents who have lost their files in "My Documents" and never found them again. "My Documents" guarantees you will have difficulty finding what you need, because it is really the same as the A to Z filing system; it requires you to remember exactly what you called that file to find it again. How does one avoid this pitfall?

Set up your computer files the same as your paper files. A friend of mine (one of those horrible, organized people) calls me the Queen of Subdirectories, but that was in the good old DOS days. In today's lingo, that would be the Queen of Folders. It is a simple concept.

> **Your computer files should be set up the same as your paper files.**

## ORDER FROM CHAOS FILE LAYOUT

In my C: directory I have a folder called "Order from Chaos." Here is where I save all my business-related work. The Order from Chaos folder only has other work folders in it. I also have a folder on my C: drive called "Canis Lupus" (I like wolves) for my personal files. It has only personal files in it. So, when I am looking for something, my first question is "Is it personal or work?" The answer tells me immediately which folder on my C: drive to *start* looking in.

Following is a simplified outline of my C: Order from Chaos directory. I have used the outline display just as you would see in directory format. I have noted which lines are folders and which are documents:

C: Order from Chaos (one of many folders under C:)

Products (folder)

Postcards (folder)

Tapes & CDs (folder)

    6-week booklet insert (document)

    6-tape marketing flyer (document)

    CD cover (document)

    Air Traffic Control (folder)

    2000 holidays (document)

    2001 holidays (document)

    future months format (document)

    cover page (document)

    Owner's manual (document)

Books (folder)

   Proposal (folder)

      Query Letter (document)

      Agent Proposal (document) (this is the proposal I created to acquire a book agent to sell this book!)

      Agents Mailing List (document)

   Book 1 (folder)

      Order from Chaos—Six Steps to Organization for the Business Person (document) (this document is this book!)

      Book in WordPerfect format (document) (my agent was using WordPerfect where I used MSWord so I saved her copy separate in case it did not get through to her)

   Random House (folder)

      Contract (document) (this is the contract for this book!)

      Administration (folder)

Humor & Inspiration (folder) (In here I keep all the funny or inspirational e-mails I get that I deem worthy of retention.)

Invoices (folder) (Each time I invoice a client I create a folder for that agency in this folder.)

KHFM (folder) (these are my radio ads)

   9812 ads (document) (these were the first ads I ran in December of 1998. My computer dude taught me to

> put the year first and the month second, using a 0 before single digit months, because then they appear in numerical order automatically. Of course 2000 screwed that up, but all the rest are in order with 00 on top.)

> 9908 ads (document) (these are the ads from August of 1999)

Training (folder)

Classes (folder)

  1 hr talks (folder)

  3 hr (folder)

  one day (folder)

  web class (folder)

  6-Week (folder) (All I have to do is go to the 6-Week folder and there is everything I might need for the class.)

    handouts (document)

    marketing flyer (document)

  rosters (document) (one from each class sorted by the date class 1 began)

  blank sign-in sheet (document)

  certificate of completion (document)

Organizations (folder):

  Chamber of Commerce (folder)

  Leadership Abq. Program (folder)

  Roundtable Program (folder)

  NAWBO (folder)

Programs Committee (folder)

Public Policy Committee (folder)

As you can see, there are indeed *many* folders within folders within folders in my computer. The advantage is I can find *anything* immediately! The only time I misplace a file is when I have accidentally saved it in the wrong folder in the first place—and that does not happen very often, or at least won't until they change the operating system again!

Remember, it is as if you were looking up a file in a physical filing cabinet (refer back to the section where we discuss setting up a physical filing system if this sounds unfamiliar).

You may have computer files where there is no corresponding paper file and vice versa. For example, my radio ads live on my computer *only*. I do not have paper copies of them. When I write a new ad, I do it on the computer and want existing ads to cannibalize. You may also have some paper-only files that are not duplicated on your computer. For example, my Pending File is paper only—I do not have a corresponding electronic Pending File. If I need to respond to some e-mail at a later time, I print it out and put it in the Pending File.

A friend of mine calls me the "Queen of Subdirectories." In today's lingo, I would have to change that to the "Queen of Folders," but it just does not have the same ring!

Take a moment now and figure out how *your* computer filing cabinet should look. Start with the "drawer" titles. Within each "drawer," identify your larger topic categories. If you have followed the system in order and created a vacuum and a Cockpit, duplicating the physical system in your electronic system should be easy.

You don't have to take all your existing computer files and put them in this new configuration. That would be far too time-consuming and tedious. Just as 95 percent of all paper over six months old is trash, 95 percent of your computer files over six months old are trash as well. Rather, create the new "drawers" and "folders" system even if they are empty. Then, as you create new files, save them in the new system. If you need an old file, open it, do what you need to with it, then save it into the new system. Eventually the new system will have all the files you really use, and the old ones can be erased, archived, or whatever is appropriate.

### 4. BOXES UNDER/AROUND THE DESK

Last, tackle the boxes of stuff under/around your desk. Like the filing cabinet, 95 percent of it will be trash. Trust me on this. I have never helped anyone sort through old papers where 95 percent did not get tossed. There will be plenty of room in the now pristine filing cabinet, bookcase, or closet to contain the 5 percent that you keep. Do you see the beauty of this method? The closer we get to current paper, the easier it is to deal with it, because the eventual receptacles for said paper are already in order with room for more.

### 5. DESK DRAWERS

Clean out each and every desk drawer. As before, do not use the hunt-and-peck method; rather, dump out the entire drawer onto a towel on the desktop. Then *intentionally* place the items you deem worthy back into the appropriate drawer. Categorize each desk drawer before refilling it. Categories might include frequently used tools, company literature/letterhead, computer supplies, personal stuff, or blank forms. Remember to group like items. People frequently find that having a "personal" drawer makes life much simpler. Rather than having your purse in one drawer, candy in another, a hairbrush in a third, and ChapStick in a fourth, consider emptying one drawer, calling it "Personal," and putting all those items in the one drawer. That way you no longer have to try to remember where things are, you *know* where they are.

The top of the desk will be addressed in the next chapter, "The Cockpit Office." I hope at this point you feel lighter, both physically and emotionally. Even though you may not be consciously aware of it, all that old stuff weighs on you. Now your office should no longer be frightening or oppressive, and you will be able to focus without the distraction of surrounding piles or the fear of not being able to find what you need.

> Now your office should no longer be frightening or oppressive. You should be without the distraction of surrounding piles or the fear of not being able to find what you need.

## CHECKLIST: CREATE A VACUUM

### WARNING!

Do NOT get bogged down in old stuff and stop the process virtually before you've started. It is more important that you deal with the new stuff as it comes in. Just make sure you have enough room in each drawer (2″ minimum) or bookcase shelf (4″ minimum) for the new stuff. If you decide to deal with the old stuff, here's the checklist.

### Vacuum Rules

1. Don't get bogged down.
2. Have these supplies ready before you start:
   - Cardboard boxes/plastic boxes with lids for storage (if using cardboard, buy a box of 10 as they are cheap and can be used for other steps later)
   - Thick, permanent marker to mark boxes clearly
   - *Huge* trashcan(s), garbage bags, recycling bins
3. Create these boxes:
   - 1 box marked To-Do Now
   - 1 box marked To-Do Later
   - boxes for archiving, appropriately categorized and labeled or awaiting labels
4. Clearly label what you archive for easy retrieval.
5. Group like objects as you archive for easy retrieval.
6. Throw away 95 percent of the old stuff.

## Start at the End, Not at the Beginning, and Work Backwards

1. Closet(s):
   - Take everything out, identifying the large categories as you go.
   - Label boxes with the identified categories.
   - Put things in the appropriate boxes.
   - Toss 95 percent, at least.

Do not be afraid of empty space.

2. Bookcase(s):
   - Empty all shelves.
   - Create categories as you remove books.
   - Categorize/label shelves.
   - Replace only items used at least once a month.
   - Anything that is outdated, duplicated, or used less often than once a month, donate/recycle/archive/toss.

3. Filing cabinet(s):

   If you have a filing system that *does* serve you:
   - Toss/archive enough old stuff to create at least two inches of play in each drawer so there is room for the new stuff when it comes in.
   - Whenever the drawer is too full to file easily, take a moment to toss/archive two inches of old stuff to make the drawer functional again.

   If you have a filing system that *does not* serve you:
   - Don't ask "how should I file this?", ask "how will I use this?"

- Identify large categories for each drawer.
- Identify larger categories within each drawer.
- Empty each drawer completely.
- Label each drawer before putting files back.
- Archive anything you have not touched in a year—just label clearly so you can find it again *if* you need it!

For computer files:

- Do not use "My Documents."
- Create a file system that mirrors your paper system with the use of folders and subfolders.
- Don't go back and move all files. Instead, use your new system from now on, and delete 95 percent of your old files.

4. Boxes/piles of stuff under and around the desk:
   - Remember, 95 percent is trash.
   - What is kept will now fit in filing cabinet/bookcase!

5. Desk drawers:
   - Identify category for each drawer and label.
   - Take everything out, then replace as needed.

6. Celebrate your newfound feeling of physical and emotional lightness!

# Step 1:
# The Cockpit Office

This step will be the longest, because the details of setting up your physical environment, your Cockpit, takes the longest to describe, but bear with me, it truly is worth it.

When you sit down at your desk to work, you need to have the tools you use *daily*, *weekly*, and *monthly* in the appropriate places. Imagine this, you are sitting at your desk, working away. You have a bill you need to pay but do not have your checkbook handy. You set the bill on the corner of your desk saying to yourself, "I'll get my checkbook and pay that bill in just a minute." Next, you type a letter to a client but do not have any letterhead handy for the printer. You say to yourself, "I'll get the letterhead in just a minute." Now you have a form you need to return. It comes with its own return envelope, but, oh dear, no stamp. Once again, "I'll just put this on the corner of the desk and get that stamp in a minute."

> When you sit down at your desk to work, you need to have the tools you use daily, weekly, and monthly in their places.

What is happening here? First, you have quite a pile of half-finished projects on the corner of your desk, which means you are going to have to, in a sense, do them again; that is, handle each of them again before they are finished. The worst aspect of this scenario is that in your brain, THESE PROJECTS ARE DONE. This is why you sometimes find things at the bottom of piles and screech aloud, "I thought this went out weeks ago!!!" See how innocently it all started?

The second danger to not having the tools we use regularly handy is how long it *actually* takes us to deal with that item that will "only take a second." In the typical situation where we interrupt *ourselves*, we take, on average, 20 minutes to actually return to the desk and the original task we interrupted ourselves for. It isn't "just a second," it is *20 minutes!* How many of those does it take to eat up your day?

Imagine a pilot. She has everything she needs right there in the cockpit to get that plane away from the gate, into the air to the destination, and back to the gate again. For example, she does not have to run to the back of the plane to put down the landing gear, does she? If she did, the drinks cart would be in the way, or at least it is whenever I need to "go to the back of the plane." How would you feel if you heard "I'm sorry, ladies and gentlemen, but we cannot land until the lady in seat 6A gets her gin and tonic with extra lime"? And yet, how often do you find yourself not paying the bill, printing the letter, or mailing the envelope because you cannot get to that last bit of equipment you need to finish the job?

What *does* happen when you get up to get that checkbook/letterhead/stamp? As soon as you stand up you say to yourself, "While I'm up I'll get a cup of coffee" or "go to the restroom" or "have a cigarette." If you have a home office, you have even *more* time-wasting opportunities, like "water that plant," "put in another load of laundry," or "walk the dog." You also run the risk of standing up to go get something and forgetting why you even stood up! Regardless of why, the "it'll just take a second" *self*-interruptions seldom take less than 20 minutes.

> Anything you use daily should be easily in hand's reach. Anything you use on a weekly basis should be in arm's reach. Anything you use monthly can be in the office. Anything used less often should be out of there!

That is why *you* need *your* cockpit customized to how *you* work and what *you* use and on what level of frequency. The formula is simple:

- **Anything you use daily should be easily in hand's reach.** Don't forget the corollary that goes, anything in hand's reach should be something you use daily.

- **Anything you use weekly should be in arm's reach** but may take more effort (i.e., behind you on a credenza, in a drawer, above you on a hutch, etc.). The trick is you should *not* have to leave your chair to get it!

- **Anything you use monthly may be in your office.** Once a month is normally the longest frequency for repetitive tasks. Once you have set up your office and you have plenty of room for the quarterly or annual tasks, consider moving them in, but *only* if you have the room. If you are only interrupting yourself once a quarter, or once a year, you can afford to waste 20 minutes for the "I'll just get another cup of coffee" routine.

- **Anything you use less often than once a month should be outside of your office.** Yes, if you live in a cubicle, this can be a real challenge. Some offices have extra storage elsewhere, closets, filing cabinets, empty offices, archive facilities, and so on. See if there is such a space for your materials.

Here is a diagram of this principle:

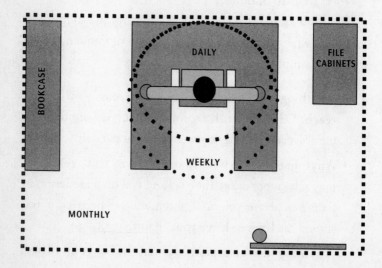

You need to set up your space based on frequency of use, not how important things are. For example, very important things (like your license to practice your profession) are virtually *never* used, but things we use daily, like company literature or sometimes even printers, are frequently quite far from our Cockpits. So how do you set up an efficient Cockpit?

## Office Layout

In a study done to identify the most *productive* environment for an office worker, the following four components were noted. The office

1. was a minimum of 10 feet by 10 feet,
2. had a door you could close,
3. had a phone you could turn off, and
4. had a minimum of 30 square feet of open desk space (that means space with nothing sitting on it—no computers, phones, lamps—just open desk space).

Does this describe your office? In all the time I've been teaching people how to get organized, only two people have actually had a space like this. The rest of the folks told horror stories. Nightmares of cubicles, bullpens, shared offices, even shared desks! My next book may be *How Employers Are Destroying Their Employees' Productivity*. In the meantime, let's

My next book may be *How Employers Are Destroying Their Employees' Productivity.*

talk about what you can do to make your space more efficient.

The most effective desk configuration is a U, as in the earlier Cockpit diagram. There are as many setups for a U as there are users. The most common setup is to place your computer (if you have one) at the bottom of the U and designate two stations, with one arm of the U for "projects" and the other arm of the U for crisis/interruptions. Project work is any task that will take you an hour or more to complete. The crisis/interruptions tasks can make up a large part of the day. They are the quick, simple tasks that take no more than a couple minutes to complete. Returning phone calls, signing papers, completing a form, faxing something, and opening the mail are a few examples.

Frequently we are working on a project, and we get interrupted. If we have only one work surface, the papers from the interruption end up on top of the papers for the project. Two or three interruptions can occur before we get back to our project. In the meantime, the project papers are now three layers down on our desk and mixed up with the three interruptions' papers. Ever wonder why you are always saying, "It was here just a minute ago"?

The interruptions' station should be the arm of the U that is closest to the door (easiest for others to reach), and the project arm should be the farthest from the door. Again, if this particular setup does not fit your personal situation, set up what does. Just do it consciously.

If you do not/cannot have a U, an L is the second-best layout, with the computer at the junction of the two arms. Again, set up the project and interruptions areas.

The third-best layout is two parallel desks, the desk in front and a credenza or table in back. The problem with this layout is your computer, as well as other tools, will be in one place and inconvenient to the second.

The least efficient layout is a straight line, like one desk or one long table. It is hard to designate stations with any reliable boundaries this way. No matter how hard you try, things seem to get mixed up.

Given most offices, furniture layout options are minimal if not impossible. Do your best. As you are setting this space up, ask yourself, "Do I need a bookcase in my Cockpit?" Most of us do not, but if your job requires you on a daily basis to have many reference books, notebooks, sample books, and so on available to you, then you *do* need a bookcase inside your Cockpit. "Do I need a filing cabinet in my Cockpit?" Most of us do not, but if you reference hundreds of client files or records daily, then you may need a filing cabinet in your Cockpit. Shared files or public files can complicate the equation; just do your best. No Cockpit is perfect, but most can be drastically improved upon.

## OPEN DESK SPACE

Now you see why an office that is at least 10 feet by 10 feet is needed. As to the 30-square-feet open desk space, we automatically know why this is necessary. When you need to do your taxes, or some other big project at home, where do you do it? Don't you head for the dining room table, clear it off, and lay out your project? The average dining room table is approximately 30 square feet. When we need to work, we *know* how much room we need. If we don't have it, we get creative. I've seen folks working on projects in little cubicles creating as much surface area as possible. They have papers in piles on the desk, drawers pulled out to act as surface area, tops of hutches used, the top of the computer used, piles on the floor around them, things balanced in their laps and under their arms. Does this work? Well, sort of. Is this efficient? No way!

Given this scenario, every square inch of surface space is precious and should not be cluttered with nonessential items. Does that mean you have to get rid of the picture of your family, or the brightly colored lump of clay your three-year-old made you? No, just get them off the desktop. The picture can hang on the wall, the "gift" can go on top of the file cabinet or wherever you have space that is not in hand's/arm's reach. Do remember to keep these mementos to a minimum. You do still need some room to work!

## INTERRUPTIONS VERSUS CONCENTRATION

Finally—about the door you can close and the phone you can turn off. The older we get, the more distractible we become; the harder it is for us to focus and concentrate. Therefore, eliminating as many interruptions and distractions as possible improves our productivity. Therefore, close the door and mute the phone. Studies have shown that a project that would take one hour to complete if you were not interrupted takes an average of four hours to complete if you *are* interrupted. What does that do to our productivity? Concentrating in a cubicle environment can be virtually impossible for some of us. Here are a couple of suggestions to improve productivity:

- Create a fake door. A chain of paper clips hung across the opening with a "Do Not Disturb" sign can help if coworkers will honor it.

- Forward your phone to someone else, or unplug it. Most voice mail systems work even with it unplugged. Check first, though.

- Do project work in a quieter space like a conference room, an empty office, or at home.

- If your office allows you to wear headphones, there is a great tool for increasing concentration—a tape or CD that plays what sounds like white noise or waves. It is designed to activate both right and left hemispheres of the brain, increasing productivity. It also drowns out surrounding noise. I am using it now as I write (I have two dogs and five cats . . . imagine the noise and distractions!). You may order one from the company Hemi-Sync at 800-541-2488 or hemisync.com on the Web. It is not expensive and very useful, especially for easily distractible folks—like me.

## Four "Must Haves" for Every Cockpit

How do you create this efficient, orderly, uninterruptible Cockpit Office? Assuming you have created a vacuum (even if it is to simply put the old stuff behind you), there should

**The four tools necessary in every Cockpit are: a Desktop File, an In Box, a To Read Box, and a To File Box.**

now be room for the stuff you *really* need. Following is a list of the items the average office needs; these four tools are necessary in each and every Cockpit:

- a Desktop File
- an In Box
- a To Read Box
- a To File Box.

Let's look at each tool and its use in greater detail.

## 1. DESKTOP FILE

We humans are basically lazy. We do whatever is the easiest—we take the path of least resistance. Therefore, being organized has got to be easier than being disorganized, or we will be disorganized. Ipso facto, the Desktop File. I'm sure you have seen one. They may look like plastic milk crates the dairies use, only better, and are designed for sitting on the top of your desk. More elegant, streamlined ones are also available; check in your office supply catalog. They are designed to hold hanging folders and are usually about 12 inches wide by 12 inches deep by 10 inches tall for letter-size paper or wider for legal size.

What do you keep in it? The Desktop File contains only *current* files that are used *daily*, or at least every other day—no less frequently than that. Likely candidates for the Desktop

File are projects you are *currently* working on, clients you are *currently* working with, references used *daily*, and/or repetitive tasks performed *daily* such as faxing. Get the idea?

**CURRENT PROJECTS/CURRENT CLIENTS** If you are currently involved in 20 different projects, the only ones that go into the Desktop File are the "hot" ones. Your involvement in those 20 projects is varied by level of activity and timing for you. Project A may be only peripheral for you. You file the weekly updates with barely a glance. For Project B, you may be the project leader, constantly answering questions, adding data, and referring to lists. Therefore, Project A would *not* be in your Desktop File, but Project B *would* be. You may have hundreds of clients, but only three with active proposals awaiting quotes or artwork or such.

**FREQUENTLY REPEATED TASKS** Another criterion for Desktop File contents would be frequently repeated tasks. If you fax many times each day, blank fax cover sheets would live in your Desktop File. Otherwise faxing requires you to run to the fax area twice (once to get a blank cover sheet and the second time to actually fax the information). With blank cover sheets in your Desktop File, you save a trip and only go once. If you use the company directory to call coworkers every day, the directory would live in your Desktop File.

> The Desktop File is a useful tool at home as well. Keep it near where you open your mail, along with a huge trashcan.

**FILE 90 PERCENT RIGHT NOW** Of the paper we save each day, 90 percent is related to something we are *currently* working on. If we could file 90 percent of our daily paper in our Desktop File *immediately*, only 10 percent would be left to be filed someplace else. That is the reason for the Desktop File. This one tool can save you tons of time and hours of frustrated scrambling for papers that were "here just a minute ago." For example, if the project file is in the filing cabinet across the room, we frequently set the newly received fax on the corner of the desk, thinking "I'll put that in the project file in just a minute." Two hours later, you run off to the project meeting, grabbing the file on the way out of the door. Once in the meeting you realize the critical information you need is in that fax still sitting on the corner of your desk—not in the project file. The Desktop File can solve these dilemmas and more.

Do not alphabetize the files in this box. There should be so few that glancing through the labels for the one you want should be a quick task. Simply put files back in the front after using them. At the end of the week, look to see which files have gravitated to the back and eliminate those by removing them from the Desktop File and putting them into the file cabinet, or wherever that category of files live. We tend to think of our lives as static, but in reality, things are changing all the time, especially the focus of our activities, which projects or clients are hot, and the frequency with which we perform certain tasks.

**SUBSTITUTING THE FILE DRAWER IN THE DESK FOR THE DESKTOP FILE** Many folks say, "But I have this drawer in my desk for files. Can't I put my most frequently used files in there?" The answer is, it depends. It depends on how lazy you are. I am *dreadfully* lazy. If I have to open that drawer to file something, I will set it on the corner of the desk above the drawer and say to myself "I'll file that in just a minute" with the best of intentions. If you are not as lazy as I am, try using the desk drawer for your hot files. If you find you do what I do, then the desk drawer will *not* work for you and you will need to get a Desktop File.

### THE DESKTOP FILE AT HOME

The Desktop File is a useful tool at home as well. Keep it near where you open your mail, along with a huge trashcan. Create categories for each pile you make when sorting your mail. Some sample categories might be:

- Bills to pay (this one is obvious)
- Things to file (like that stuff the insurance company sends you that is not part of the bill. You don't know what it is for, but you are afraid to throw it away for fear you may need it some day. Or all those statements the bank and the investment company sends you.)
- Things to read (this includes newsletters from organizations in your private life, favorite magazines, and such)
- Things to take to the office (you need to transfer this to a place where it will actually get taken to the office at some point)
- One for each family member (here you can put private correspondence, individual bills, and homework left lying around)

When a category gets too full, "things to file" for example, take the contents to your filing cabinet and file them. If you do need something that you know you received but it is not in the file, it will be in the "to file" section, and you will still find it.

The exception to this practice would be things that arrive in huge volume, such as catalogs. Most of us get *way* too many catalogs. I keep mine on the back of the toilet. It is a self-limiting stack—anything much over six inches starts to slide around. Then I just take the bottom half and toss them, leaving the most current on top. Perhaps you peruse catalogs while watching television, or in bed. Wherever you read them, keep them there, once again, with a huge trashcan for tossing or recycling them when you are done. Another method for catalogs is to say "Do I have any extra money to buy stuff now?" If the answer is no, just toss/recycle the catalogs. Why are you torturing yourself looking at things you cannot afford, anyway?

**TRAVELERS OR MULTIPLE OFFICES** If you frequently travel with your work, you may want to get a Desktop File with a lid and a handle so you can take it with you. If you have multiple offices, I recommend one Desktop File for each office. Decide which tasks you will perform at each office. Keep them as separate as possible. For the few things you absolutely

A method for dealing with all those catalogs is to ask yourself, "Do I have any extra money to buy stuff now?" If the answer is no, just toss the catalogs.

must do at both, keep those files in the traveling Desktop File along with two files called "To Office A" and "To Office B." If you receive something in Office A that belongs in Office B, you have a simple method to get it there. Never *ever* have two files with the same name, as that guarantees that whatever you need will be in the other file in the other office.

Next, let's consider the other three necessary tools for each and every Cockpit Office. They are three stacking trays. There are many varieties of stacking trays available, from inexpensive plastic to exotic (expensive) woods. The only difference is the look; the functionality is the same. Stack the In, To Read, and To File trays on top of each other with the In tray on top. You may add other trays to this stack later, but In is always the top one as it has the potential to be the most frequently used and contain the most stuff.

> **Everybody needs a place for "in." We need a way to keep the new stuff and the old stuff from getting all mixed up together.**

## 2. THE IN BOX

Everybody needs a designated place for "in." We need a way to keep the *new stuff we get* and the *old stuff we have* from getting mixed up together. We get into trouble when we find a "new" thing at the bottom of a bunch of "old" things. It impairs our efficiency and adds to our stress. Other people need to know where to put new stuff for you as well, rather than putting it on your chair or taping it to your phone, or handing it to you in the hallway because they are afraid if they put it on your desk it will simply disappear along with everything else that has ever gone into your office. The solution to both these dilemmas is the In Box.

What goes into the In Box? *Everything new.* New mail, new phone messages, new faxes, new information from others, anything you have not yet seen, reviewed, or dealt with. Other people put things in your In Box, but so do you. If you return from a meeting with a project file full of things for you to follow up on, but you have to run off to the next meeting before you can deal with them, put the file in your In Box for later review. The tasks represented in it are *new* to you and therefore qualify. If you just set the file, and its represented tasks, on the desk, it may get shoved aside, buried, or forgotten. Forgotten also will be the tasks, until the next meeting when someone asks you, "So, what progress did you make on X?" and you realize you totally forgot about X until that moment. Not good!

There are two In Box rules.

**IN BOX RULE #1** Allot a *minimum* of one hour each day just to deal with the new information you receive. We immediately think of the physical In Box, but you have many other *virtual* In Boxes. For example, there are e-mails, faxes, voice mail, cell phone messages, pages, and so on. And don't forget your *portable* In Boxes, such as your purse, your briefcase, your knapsack, the passenger seat of your car—all those places *new* stuff collects.

> Allot a *minimum* of one hour each day just to deal with the new information you receive.

You must empty each and every one of them *at least* once every 24 hours. We will talk more about just how to make the decisions and what to do with the paper as we go. For now, just allot the hour of time.

When you deal with all your In Boxes depends on you. If you are a morning person, dealing with the new may be a task best accomplished first thing when you are sharp and alert. If you are a night person, dealing with the new may be best left to the end of the day. Either way, try to be as consistent about the time as you can. The more you make it a repetitive habit, the easier it is to do.

**IN BOX RULE #2** The second In Box rule is that you do not get to take something out of your In Box, say "I don't know what to do with this," and put it back in the In Box,

> **When you have more than one In Box's depth of things to read, all you have is a stack of guilt!**

or leave it in the new messages of your e-mail, or save the message and leave it on the machine. Once you take it out, read it, or listen to it, it *must* go someplace else. As this section progresses, you will begin to know where those places are. For now, just know every In Box must be totally empty once each day.

### 3. THE TO READ BOX

Directly under the In Box is the To Read Box. The amount of stuff that can go into the To Read Box is limited by the bottom of the In Box. This is a good thing. The usual space between the bottom of the To Read Box and the bottom of the

In Box is about two and one-half inches. A two-and-one-half-inch stack of stuff to read is sufficient for most of us.

We all get information we think we would like to read someday. We seldom actually get around to reading much of it, but hope springs eternal. This material to read is coming in faster than we can read it, and much of it is really just trash, if we were realistic. Consider this—we get more mail in a day than our parents got in a week and than our grandparents got in a year! A huge amount of it is material to read: trade journals, reports, magazines, newsletters, flyers, brochures, and articles, not to mention pure junk mail. It all goes into the To Read Box. When the To Read Box is so full you could not fit another sheet of tissue paper into it, it is time to purge.

What do you purge? The things that have been put into the To Read Box range in importance from 1 (trivial) to 10 (critical). We do not make that distinction when we put them into the box. When we are putting them in, they all *seem* vital to continued life on this planet. In reality their importance varies greatly. For example, your professional journal is probably the most important piece of reading material you receive. A 1 would be yet another offer for 10 CDs for only a penny. If you never open the CD flyer, nothing will happen, except that you will save time each month *not* checking the "do not send this month's selection" box and putting a stamp on it.

How do you purge? Take everything out of the To Read Box, fan it across your desk, and look for the three (at most five) most important pieces. Put those three to five back in the To Read Box, and throw the rest in the trash. "I can't just toss those priceless treasures," you wail. Well, you *must*, because I promise you it is coming in faster than you can read it. If you have more than a three-inch pile of things to read, what you have is a stack of *guilt*. Whenever you look at the pile, you feel overwhelmed, inadequate, and out of control. Why would you intentionally create something that makes you feel bad? No matter how guilty you feel, it is still coming in faster than you can read it. The only solution is to purge!

I had one client who liked to read the *Wall Street Journal.* It was delivered every day to his office. On average, he read the *Journal* three times a week. When he did not get around to reading it, he put it aside on a table in his office, promising himself he would read it later. When I arrived to help him get organized, he had a stack of *Wall Street Journal*s over five feet tall! I asked him how often he read the *Journal.* "About three times a week." "Do you ever read more than one in a day?" I asked. "Oh, no. Never," he replied. "Then what IS that?" I asked, pointing to his Mt. Everest of old *Wall Street Journal*s. It was a MOUNTAIN of guilt. They reminded him of money he had paid and not utilized. They reminded him that he was WAY behind in his reading. They made him feel overwhelmed, behind, and out of control! I suggested, "Throw the #@$&% things out!" To this day, he still calls me to tell me how he is still throwing his unread *Wall Street Journal*s away.

The exception to the two-and-one-half-inch rule is if it is your *job description* to read stuff (like my book agent or my editor, for example). For the majority of us, reading is relatively inconsequential to our real jobs.

There is a way to increase your time available to read. Try putting a couple pieces from your To Read Box in your purse/briefcase each day. During the day we all have those inevitable times of waiting. You know, at the doctor's office, in line at the grocery, in a boring meeting, while waiting for a client, when the freeway turns into a parking lot. You can sit and fume that the doctor/client/clerk is keeping you waiting, or you can say, "Oh goodie! I can read that article I brought." The end result is you are actually a tiny bit disappointed when the doctor/client/clerk finally does get to you, rather than fuming and tapping your foot impatiently with a scowl on your face.

### 4. THE TO FILE BOX

We all have things that come to us that we need to keep but do not need *inside* our Cockpit; that is, they are not used *daily* or *weekly*. For example, insurance companies seem to excel at sending out a plethora of paper that we cannot understand but *must* keep—it says so. Hopefully we will never need these papers, but we save them (just like we don't remove those "do not remove" tags on our pillows and mattresses). Therefore, these papers need to go someplace other than in our Cockpit, but *not right now*. We don't want to jump up and run around putting these things away immediately. We also do not want to pile them on the corner of the desk, now do we?

Magazines are a special bugaboo of mine. First, ask yourself, how many magazines do I *actually* read each month? For most of us, it is at most two or three. Now, how many magazines do you have a subscription to? More like five or ten? Pick your favorite two or three (whatever the number you actually do read) and cancel the subscriptions to the others. "But, I might miss something important," you shriek. Guess what . . . you already *are* "missing it" because you never read those other seven magazines anyway. Plus they add to your sense of being overwhelmed and out of control. I don't even want to mention the money you are wasting. Get out of fairyland where you are a person of leisure with plenty of time to read everything that interests you and join the land of reality where your leisure reading time is *very* limited!

For dealing with the magazines you *do* keep subscriptions to, I recommend that you open them with razor blade in hand, search the table of contents for articles you want to read, cut them out, staple each article separately, and throw the rest of the magazine away.

Tell me if this sounds familiar. You have something that needs to be filed but you feel rushed and don't have time to file it right now. You put it on top of the filing cabinet saying to yourself, with all sincerity, "I'll file that in just a moment." The next thing you come across that needs to be filed goes on top of the first piece of paper on top of the filing cabinet and you say, still in all sincerity, "I'll file

> **We don't want to jump up and run around filing every piece of paper immediately. We also do not want to pile them on the corner of the desk.**

both of those in just a moment." Weeks/months later, when the pile on top of the filing cabinet is so high it has become unstable, you shove it back against the wall for extra structural integrity. Then your eye lights on the virgin space in front of the supported pile and you begin yet another "I'll file that in just a moment" stack (at this point you probably do not believe yourself anymore, but you still do it).

I have a filing cabinet in my office but not *in* my Cockpit. I also have this box labeled To File *in* my cockpit. That is where these papers live, until I file them. If you need something from your archives, it will be in one of two places—in the archives or in the To File Box. Given just two places to look, I can find anything. Again, it is below the To Read Box so how high the pile can get is limited. If it gets too high, as in our structurally unstable example above, we go into over-whelmed mode, then never quite seem to get around to it.

> **If you need something from your archives, it will be in one of two places, in the archives or in the To File Box. Given just two places to look, I can find anything.**

How often should you file? As soon as your To File Box is full. That may be daily, weekly, or monthly. Personally, I file when I have to go into it to find something, then I file it all. Some folks, like those in the medical field, have things that *must* be filed by the end of the day. For them I recommend two To File Boxes—one for To File Today and one for To File

Eventually. We don't want you getting sued, or for Mr. Johnson to miss his medication, now do we?

Remember, if you can get a copy of the item you are thinking about keeping and filing from someplace else, DON'T KEEP IT! People who write memos, reports, and minutes are *very* proud of them. They believe everybody else's reports/minutes are boring, but *theirs* are utterly riveting. If you need another copy of what they created, they will be absolutely *thrilled* that you asked and more than happy to mail/fax/e-mail/hand-carry you another copy. So let them keep track of it.

> **If you can get a copy of the item you are thinking about keeping and filing from someplace else ... DON'T KEEP IT!**

On the next page is a little flowchart for you to help you decide what to save and where to save it.

## The Rest of the Tools in Your Cockpit

### ENORMOUS WASTEBASKET

Most folks throw away *far* too little. This is a human nature thing. We have some sort of strange relationship to paper. Somehow, having a specific piece of paper makes us feel secure, as if just having that piece of paper guarantees we won't forget, or we have the knowledge or our #@$%*'s are covered. Well, that is simply not true. Ninety-five percent of the stuff that is cluttering up my clients' desks winds up going into the trash by the end of our sessions. Notice how many of the things you

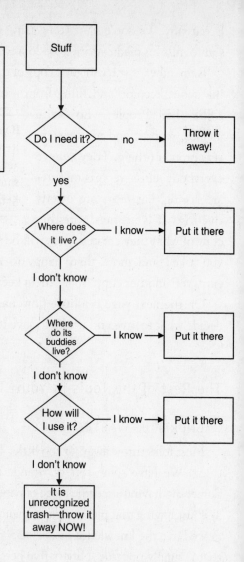

save way past their prime end up in the trash eventually anyway. Why delay their progress to the landfill or the recycling bin? Just throw them away! You are more likely to pitch things if you have a huge yawning trashcan mouth begging to be filled, as opposed to a dainty, color-coordinated, frou-frou wastebasket that matches your hair barrettes, or whatever.

## CRUMPLED VERSUS UNCRUMPLED

I remember something my fifth-grade teacher taught us and I will pass it along to you. Crumpled-up paper takes up way more room in the trash than a nice flat uncrumpled piece of paper does. She divided the class in half, gave each of us one piece of paper and placed two empty trashcans at the head of the class. The half of the class on the right was to crumple their papers before tossing them. The other half was to toss their papers in pristine and uncrumpled. We marched past our appropriate trashcan, single file, tossing as instructed. When we were done, we filed past again to notice the results. The trashcan with the crumpled paper was full, while the uncrumpled receptacle was barely one-tenth full. That little lesson has stayed with me all these years. Now it can haunt you as well!

## PENCIL HOLDER

Everyone needs some repository on top of the desk to hold the items used daily or every other day. Those tools need to be on top of your desk, not in a drawer. I am talking about some exquisite pencil holder that matches your expensive desk set

## SHREDDED VERSUS UNSHREDDED

Regarding shredding versus not shredding.... I suggest not shredding. It is time-consuming and if "they" want to get you, they don't need to go through your trash to do it. There was a program on one of the afternoon talk shows where they took two volunteers from the audience who were listed in the phone book. They went backstage with a couple computer hackers, supplying the hackers with nothing more than their names and addresses as they appeared in the phone book. After an alarmingly short period of time they came back on stage. The hackers had the two audience members' social security numbers, bank account numbers and balances, and credit card numbers, balances, and limits. They had much more information than that, but that is what I remember. Given that, if "they" want you, "they" will get you with or without you shredding.

How many times do you pick out a pen, find that it does not write, then put it *back* in your pencil holder and search for yet another pen? From this day forward, if it doesn't work, just THROW IT AWAY!

or some kind of old coffee cup, plastic glass, or something your kids made you, which is what most of us have. The reason it needs to be on *top* of your desk is for efficiency. If you need, for example, your favorite red pen, how long does it take you to open a drawer, fumble around in the drawer looking for a favorite (which somehow always seems to drift to the bottom of the pile), get it out, use it, and then put it away again when you are done? An extra 30 seconds, maybe? If you spend an extra 30 seconds three times *each day* getting out and putting back the pens/pencils/scissors/rulers, and so on, that you use regularly, how many minutes does that add up to in a day, a week, a month, a year? It may not seem like much, but it really adds up!

Make sure the tools in your pencil cup are the ones you *like*, the ones you *use*, and the ones that *actually work!* How many times do you pick out a pen that does not write, or a pencil that is not sharpened, only to put it back and search for another? When that happens, pitch it or sharpen it, but *don't* just put it back. Keep only the tools you *like* to write with there. How many times do you push aside the junky pens you hate, fiddling around, looking for your favorite pen? Get rid of the yucky ones, and just have your favorites. Sort out the ones you constantly shove aside and put them in the supply closet. You'd be surprised how often the pens you hate are someone else's favorite!

If you have more than one pencil holder on your desk, you know what I am going to say, right? You just need one. All the others must go. If you think it wastes your time looking through one pencil cup for your favorite pen, imagine how long it takes if you have three or four (no, that many is *not* unusual).

## FILE FOLDERS/HANGING FOLDERS

Keep at least a month's supply of extras on hand, so you can add files and categories as needed. Keep a few in the back of each file drawer and a few in the back of your desktop file.

Otherwise, if you need to start a new file, you will set the future contents on the corner of your desk, telling yourself "I'll get a file folder in just a minute." Yeah, sure. Always buy plenty before starting a cleaning-out job, since old ones may need to be replaced. If you use a color code with your files, make sure you have extras of each color on hand. If you need a red and only have pink, you may be tempted to say "Pink is sort of reddish" and therefore compromise your system. If colored folders themselves are too much trouble, consider just color coding the labels with a highlighter.

**Keep at least a month's supply of extra folders on hand, so you can add files and categories as needed.**

## ROLODEX AND BLANK CARDS

I recommend a full circle Rolodex (where you turn the wheel and it spins) that holds $3'' \times 5''$ cards rather than a flat Rolodex. A flat Rolodex becomes a pile of napkins, Post-it notes, matchbook covers, corners torn off envelopes and business cards in no time. At least the round ones can't have things piled on top of them.

One day my accountant said to me, "You need to call Ms. X," and turned to her flat Rolodex for the number. She hesitated in front of the mound of bits, scraps, and who knows what else, then turned to pull out her phone book. "Don't you have her number in your Rolodex?" I queried. "It's faster to look it up in the book" was her response. Does this describe *your* system? Needless to say, she received a 360-degree Rolodex for Christmas from me that year (shopping for my disorganized friends is so easy).

To begin, take all the business cards, scraps of paper, old matchbooks, napkins, Post-it notes, whatever you currently have, and staple each to a 3″ × 5″ Rolodex card. Then, file each under the appropriate letter, but don't bother to alphabetize them, just get all the S's together, and so on. This should take no longer than 20 to 30 minutes. You can even have your child do it, as my accountant did. Every time you come in with another new business card, Post-it, or scrap, just staple it onto a card and add to the collection.

> You don't have to file every business card you get by the person's last name. If you are as bad at names as I am, that is a sure way to have a totally useless Rolodex.

Once it is set up, whenever you use a number, pull the card out of its current location and place it in the front. Eventually your most used numbers will be in the front. Is this the most efficient system? No. It is a simple, easy, hassle-free system that you *will* use.

Another note about Rolodexes—you don't have to file every business card you get by the person's last name. If you are as bad at names as I am, that is a sure way to have a totally useless Rolodex. In my Rolodex I have added extra tabs. You can get them at any office supply and just stick on to an existing card in the Rolodex. You write your own title on the tab. I have added tabs for each organization, frequently used category, and special event where I get business cards.

When I meet someone, I staple their business card at the back of the appropriate organization/event where I met them. Even though I am horrible with names, I can usually remember *where* I met someone, *how recently,* and *what* they do. That gives me three pieces of information about the person I am looking for and, with whatever else I remember about them, increases the odds I will find them again. If I just filed them alphabetically by their last name, I promise you I would neither recognize who any given card represented nor be able to find them if I needed them.

**ELECTRONIC VERSUS PAPER ROLODEXES** There are many electronic tools available to replace the old paper system. If you want to use an electronic system, *and you will spend the time to keep it current,* then use one. I have heard many horror stories from folks who had their electronic system fail, losing all their information. Electronic systems are smaller, lighter, and more fun to play with. Unless you can dock it with a larger system to back up your information, however, it is very risky. Even having a backup can be a problem if your system catches a virus. Paper systems are still quicker, if bulkier. The decision is yours. All my phone/address tracking systems are paper. My mailing list is computerized, but I have paper backup so it could be retyped, if necessary.

## PHONE BOOKS/ORGANIZATIONAL DIRECTORIES

I keep the *most recent* phone books, both white pages and yellow pages, on a shelf above my computer in my Cockpit, because I use them at least once a week. I keep with them the *most recent* copies of my organizational directories because it

I keep the *most recent* copies of my organizational directories in my Cockpit because I am always needing someone's e-mail, zip code, or company name.

seems I am always needing someone's e-mail, zip code, or company name. I actually use my organizational directories more often than the regular phone book.

## NOTE CARDS/THANK-YOU NOTES

I include note cards and thank-you notes because in our highly mechanized, technological culture we have gotten away from many manual tasks. Think back on the last time your received recognition for something. What meant more to you, the "way to go" e-mail, or the handwritten note card with the article cut out from the paper included? I doubt you still have the e-mail, but I bet you still have the card. Handwritten notes, whether to congratulate someone or to thank them, is a tradition we should not lose. So I keep mine handy.

I once heard about a lovely tradition you might want to start, too. The person wrote one thank-you note each day. It was always written to someone who had been kind, gone out of their way, or pleasantly surprised the sender. You know how you feel when you receive such a note. Other folks feel the same way. What a special way to brighten up the world.

Another tradition you may want to start is keeping a "warm fuzzy" file. Mine is in my filing cabinet and contains all those nice notes I have received from grateful clients, friends congratulating me on some accomplishment, or sayings that just make me feel better. Whenever I am feeling down (or for you entrepreneurs out there, on those days when you wonder, "Why don't I go get a *real* job?"), I open up my warm fuzzy file and after just a few minutes I am myself again, only better.

STAMPS OF VARIOUS DENOMINATIONS,
A POSTAGE SCALE, AND A POSTAGE RATES CHART

Many folks have a mail department, or a postage meter, so stamps are not an issue. If you do your own mailing (or for at home), this is another *real* time saver. How often do you put something into an envelope and wonder whether one stamp is enough? How about sending something in a 9″ × 12″ manila envelope—how many stamps does that take? I have a cheap little scale (the type often used for food weighing) that I keep in my Cockpit, along with normal letter stamps, extra-ounce stamps, oversize stamps, and postcard stamps. I send out my promotional pens frequently, and the bubble-wrap-lined 5″ × 7″ envelope I use, plus one sheet of notepaper and one pen, costs exactly 56 cents to mail, so I have 56-cent stamps as well. Just a little forethought can save *tons* of time standing in lines at the post office.

## Customizing Your Cockpit

What do *you* need that is not on the "rest of the tools in your Cockpit" list? Here is the test: If you have to get up to get something to finish a job, bring it back with you and keep it in your Cockpit. If it belongs to someone else, buy one of your own and keep it in your Cockpit.

If you use a tool in two places in your Cockpit and cannot reach it easily from both spots, buy a second. For me it was scissors. I need a pair where I write, and I also need one next to my computer. I spent $2.50 and bought a second pair of scissors and no longer interrupt my "flow," and I decreased the "now where did I put those scissors?" moments as well as simply increasing my speed of access.

Sometimes it is difficult to figure out what you use and what you don't use, so here is a quick trick. For one week, every time you use something, put a fluorescent sticky note on it. At the end of the week, review what has sticky notes and what does not. You may be surprised at the results. We seldom have a clear idea of how things really are, and we are full of assumptions. Unless it was a truly unusual week, you should be able to move out of hand's reach anything you didn't put a sticky note on. The rest can go either in arm's reach (weekly use), elsewhere in the office (monthly use), or out of there (less than monthly use). Following is a list of potential items for your Cockpit. Do not use this as a "fill-up-my-Cockpit-with" list, but rather as a pick-and-choose list. Remember, when it comes to your space, less is better!

> **If you have to get up to get something to finish a job, bring it back with you and keep it in your Cockpit.**

## "STUFF YOU MAY NEED IN YOUR COCKPIT" LIST

❑ *comfortable* chair (if you are uncomfortable or tired, work takes longer to complete. Save time—get comfortable!)

❑ good light (adjustable lamp if needed)

❑ clock

❑ paper stand/holder for typing ease

❑ business stationery, second sheets, and envelopes

❑ other special paper (mailing labels, colored paper, certificate paper, etc.)

❑ return address labels/address stamp

❑ mail labels

❑ telephone (on the left if you are right-handed, the right if you are left-handed, headset if you are tied to it)

❑ computer, typewriter, fax, printer, scanner, copier (i.e., the appropriate technology)

❑ replacement cartridges for the above technology

❑ mouse pad, wrist rest, foot rest (i.e. tools for proper ergonomics)

❑ floppy disks/Zip disks/Jaz disks/blank CDs

❑ stapler

❑ staple remover

❑ tape (regular, double-sided, masking, duct, whatever)

❑ rubber bands

❑ paper clips

❑ correction fluid/correction tape

- ❏ calculator
- ❏ hole punch
- ❏ reference manuals
- ❏ pen/pencil refills
- ❏ scratch paper/sticky notes (in a drawer, not on the desktop)
- ❏ calendar

## CHECKLIST: THE COCKPIT OFFICE

### Rules of the Cockpit Office

1. Set up your office based on frequency of use.
   - Anything you use daily should be in hand's reach.
   - Anything that is in hand's reach should be something you use daily.
   - Anything you use weekly should be in arm's reach.
   - Anything that is in arm's reach should be something you use weekly.
   - Anything you use monthly should be in the office.
   - Anything that is in the office should be something you use monthly.
   - If you use it less often than once a month, try to keep it elsewhere.

2. The ideal office layout has these qualities.
   - 10′ × 10′.
   - A door you can close.
   - A phone you can turn off.
   - A minimum of 30 square feet of open desk space.
   - A U is the best layout.
   - An L is the next best layout.
   - Two parallel surfaces are better than one surface.
   - A straight line is the least efficient layout.

3. If you need to concentrate, try to eliminate interruptions or move to a place where you can eliminate interruptions.

4. Acquire and label these tools:
   - Desktop "hot" File.
     - Fill with files used daily or every other day.
     - This includes current projects/clients.
     - This includes frequently repeated tasks.
     - You may use the desk file drawer for the Desktop File, *if you use it*. If not, get a desktop variety.
   - In Box
     - Allot a minimum of one hour each day to deal with the new incoming.
     - Nothing that comes out of the In Box can go back in—you have to find some other home for it.
     - Tell others where it is.
     - Empty it at least once every 24 hours.

- Includes all virtual In Boxes as well: e-mail, fax, voice mail, briefcase/knapsack/purse, passenger seat of car
- To Read Box
- To File Box
- Use the tools list to stock your Cockpit.

5. Sort miscellaneous items into appropriate categories:
- Desktop File
- In Box
- To Read
- To File
- Client files
- Project files
- Archives

# Step 2:
# Air Traffic Control

We all live complicated lives, and we have tons of things we must remember to do; personal errands and favors, professional tasks, long-term project responsibilities, civic obligations, religious responsibilities, family duties. These are what make up the 190 pieces of information the average businessperson receives each day. We created a Cockpit to house the accompanying paper, but now how do we keep track of it all? How do we make sure everything gets done on time, nothing is forgotten, and we stay on track with as little stress and frustration as possible? Air Traffic Control—that's how.

Here is the Air Traffic Control, single radar screen for each day's solution in a nutshell:

> Write **everything** down!
> Write it all down in **the same place.**
> Write it all down in a **time-sensitive manner.**

**Air Traffic Control is one single radar screen for each individual day.**

The purpose of Air Traffic Control is to have *one single radar screen* for each day. You need one screen where you have everything you need to do that day, just as traffic controllers have one single radar

> I would be lost without my Air Traffic Controller, because I am disorganized, and I can't remember a thing.

screen for all the planes they are currently responsible for. The things you must be able to see on your radar screen are

- appointments, set out in the hours of the day;
- to-do's listed with an easy way to prioritize them; and
- related notes, such as maps to where you are going, agenda items you thought of before the meeting, ideas you have come up with, phone numbers you needed to quickly jot down, design layouts, and so on.

I have used an Air Traffic Controller for more than 15 years. I would be lost without it because I am a disorganized person, and I know from many embarrassing experiences that I can't remember a thing for longer than 30 seconds, and sometimes not even that long. I have too many to-do's and too small an office to leave something out to remind me, and a single to-do list does not begin to *efficiently* manage all the things I already know I need to do days, weeks, months, even years, from now. Take a look at a sample from *my* Air Traffic Controller:

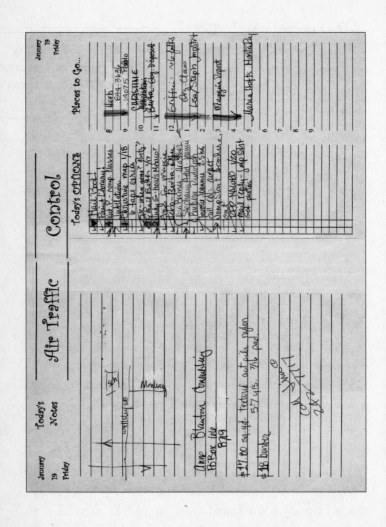

How *do* we handle all those items that have no piece of paper attached to them? Sticky notes, of course. Those go on the desktop, stuck along the front of the hutch, along the edges of the computer monitor, on the bulletin board, on the phone, on your calendar, on your sun visor, in your wallet.

> The average human can only keep seven things in short-term memory. How many are you carrying right now?

## Why Do I Want an Air Traffic Controller?

The importance of Air Traffic Control is to get things *out of your head and down on paper* in a timely fashion so that when it is time to act on them they will be waiting for you. Having a calendar-based system allows you to schedule tasks and reminders on *the appropriate day*. That way, you do not have to look at everything you need to do until the end of time, something that would overwhelm any of us. You only need to look at things you need to act on *today*—your single radar screen.

### ELIMINATING THE "LEAVE SOMETHING OUT TO REMIND ME" SYSTEM

When it comes to the piles on your desk, Air Traffic Control helps clean up that mess. If you have been using the "out of sight, out of mind method" and leaving papers out to remind you of stuff, you can now completely eliminate that system. Write down the information in the Air Traffic Controller on the appropriate radar screen to remind you, then file the paper where it belongs in your Cockpit. It is that simple. Air Traffic

## HOW DID I GET IN MY CURRENT MESS?

The average human can only keep seven things in short-term memory. I don't know about you, but I have more than seven things to remember before breakfast! It seems as though we can remember more than seven, but that is because we are always shifting around the items in those seven slots in our short-term memory.

Suppose you have seven things you are keeping in your head, then your spouse calls and asks you to bring home a quart of milk. "No problem" you say, believing you now have *eight* things in your short-term memory basket. WRONG! You still only have seven; one of the others just fell out. You won't realize this, of course, until you see that person or get that phone call or attend that meeting, and then you will say, "*%#$*! I could have sworn I was remembering that."

There is also a direct correlation between memory and stress; that is, the more stressed we are, the less we can remember. What happens when you forget something? Your stress level goes up. Now you are more stressed, which means you can keep fewer things in short-term memory. Therefore you just forgot something else, and so on and so on. Eventually you will not remember your own name and have a nervous breakdown! Therefore, remembering is *not* a good method. It is the least reliable and the most stressful.

Once we realize remembering does not work (this usually after forgetting something *really* important and getting in mucho trouble), we progress to the single most common method I see being used by office people today. That method is the "I'll leave something out on my desk to remind me" method. Yes, it is better than remembering, but with 190 pieces of information coming at us each day, the piles get really high really quick.

Incoming information does not arrive in an organized manner. Today you will receive some things you need to do today. Fine. But you will also receive some things you need to do tomorrow. Okay. But what about the things you need to do next week, or next month, or six months from now? Where do those go? Eventually, things we need to do today are all mixed up with things we need to do tomorrow and next week and next month. We look at the piles and we know there are things we need to do in there, we just don't know *what* they are or remember *where* they are. How's that for stress inducing?

Control replaces the 500 floating pieces of paper: sticky notes, backs of envelopes, and odd scraps with pertinent data on them, reports, agendas, meeting notices, and copies of things you lost once already. You can make notes for agenda items for meetings as the ideas come to you, whether you are at home, in the grocery store, or having lunch with a friend.

You will be amazed at how many of the pieces of paper lying around can simply be thrown away once you have written down what they were

One of the best ways to become religious about writing everything down is to tell your friends, family members, coworkers, and boss that if they do not see you write it down, it won't get done.

there to remind you of. Much of that clutter was simply because you knew you could not trust your memory for something due days or weeks from now. Now, your memory is no longer a player. It is Air Traffic Control ONLY and nothing else.

### HAVING WHAT YOU NEED WHEN AND WHERE YOU NEED IT

You can have maps to places you need to go handy and where you need them when you need them. How many times have you driven off toward some destination only to realize the sticky note the directions are on is someplace other than with you? And you have a place to jot down your random ideas that you may want to act on later when you're not driving, or talking on the phone, or in a movie.

### ONE LIFE, ONE SYSTEM

A common question people ask me is, "Do you have a different book for your personal life?" My answer is an emphatic NO. I have one life, so I have one book. As soon as you have more than one system, you have just doubled the odds that you will miss something.

### LEGAL DOCUMENTATION

There is one last reason to use an Air Traffic Controller— legal documentation. I have been using an Air Traffic Control system for almost 20 years, and I have archived all pages for each year. I have been told it is my best defense in case the IRS ever audits me. I also have been told by more than one source that the IRS is looking for people without systems,

## THE DISORGANIZED AIR TRAFFIC CONTROLLER

Imagine an air traffic controller who managed her air space the way most office people manage theirs. What if she kept track of the planes this way:

- Some of the planes were on a computer screen.
- Some planes she kept track of on a note pad.
- Some planes she would just remember.
- Some planes were represented by sticky notes on the edge of the computer monitor.
- A few planes were represented by papers in her briefcase.
- Some planes were represented by papers left in the passenger seat of her car.
- The rest were represented by pieces of paper in piles on her desk and on the floor.
- The planes she was responsible for today were mixed with planes that are not due until tomorrow or the next day, or a week from now.

Would you want to fly into that airport? Not on your life, literally! You wouldn't even want to fly there if you knew the air traffic controller had *two* different systems to keep track of planes, would you? The insanity of that method is so obvious, and yet it is the method most of us use when trying to keep track of what we need to do each day.

people who are guessing or making up numbers. As soon as it is obvious you have a system and are not making up clients and mileage out of thin air, they tend to back off (no, I am not requesting an audit, thank you).

I have also been told it is a legally admissible document in court. Why would that be? Because it is a *system*. Who would you believe, a person who presented you with something scratched on the back of an envelope, or a person who pulled out his or her Air Traffic Controller, flipped to the exact date, and read out what was noted there? I would believe the person with the system, not the person with notes on trash.

## How to Create Air Traffic Control from Where You Are Now

So how do you go from Chaos to Order? Follow these simple steps. Just make sure you leave enough time to complete each step uninterrupted.

### 1. ACQUIRE/CREATE AN AIR TRAFFIC CONTROL SYSTEM

An Air Traffic Controller is simply dated pages in a ring binder, usually 5.5″ wide by 8.5″ tall. Numerous systems are available. An effective system has two necessary characteristics:

1. There are two pages for each day.
2. There is a way to plan months and years into the future.

People frequently say they like to see a week at a glance, or a month at a glance. To them I say, "Thanks for sharing, now get a system with two pages for each day." The week at a glance format does not allow for a single radar screen. It doesn't have enough room to write all tasks you need to accomplish in a given day, nor does it have room for notes. It makes you write down only the most important tasks, leaving the rest to become piles, sticky notes, and things to remember. Yes, sometimes a bigger view would be more convenient, but if it does not work for everything, requiring secondary systems, why do it? The same is true for month at a glance, only more so.

> **Write everything down!
> Write it all down in the same place.
> Write it all down in a time-sensitive manner.**

You can order an official Order from Chaos Air Traffic Controller on my website (see the Resources section at the end of the book). The advantage to the original Air Traffic Controller is it is the only one designed for the 90 percent of us who are right-handed. You also can go to your local office supply and get one. Many other companies make them, including Day Runner, Franklin Covey, and Day-Timer.

You can even make your own Air Traffic Controller by getting a journal or a spiral notebook and numbering *ahead of time* the upper right-hand corner with the month, day, year, and day of the week, as in Tuesday, January 14, 2002. You must date all the pages in the book so you know how to find next Monday or the third Tuesday

> **You can make your own Air Traffic Controller by getting a journal or a spiral notebook and dating the pages *ahead of time*.**

of next week easily for future tasks, appointments, and notes. Leave the last page without a date and simply write "future" on it, so you can make a note of anything that will need to be acted upon on some date not encompassed by the current book. When you make the next book, transfer all the "future" tasks, appointments, and notes at that time.

## 2. GATHER TOGETHER ALL YOUR CURRENT TRACKING SYSTEMS

You need to identify how many different systems you use now. Most folks I work with have at least two and often three systems. I've even seen folks use as many as eight different systems. The most common examples of other systems include:

- small calendars in your purse or briefcase
- desk pad calendars
- wall calendars for vacations, sick leave, conferences
- company monthly calendars
- family calendars on the fridge at home
- notes in a computer system
- paper pads where people take notes at meetings and during phone conversations
- notes or papers in project or client files
- the piles on the desk
- the piles on the floor
- stacking trays with names
- stacking trays without names
- sticky notes
- bulletin boards

- asking someone else to remind you
- things stuck above the sun visor in the car
- notes on the bathroom mirror
- e-mails/voice mails requiring action that have not been deleted

How many of those systems are you using? With that many systems, something is practically guaranteed to get overlooked. Not to mention all the time and stress required to check them all and not forget one. You need *one* radar screen, and one radar screen only. Therefore, gather them all together, sit down with them and your new Air Traffic Controller, and begin putting them all in the one system.

> To remember to take my Air Traffic Controller with me everywhere, I made it my purse by personalizing what I carry in it.

### 3. ENTER EVERYTHING IN YOUR AIR TRAFFIC CONTROLLER

Don't just start writing down everything to do on today or tomorrow's list, or you will fill up with the first things you come to, not necessarily the most important things. For a first-time activity, write all the tasks you identify on a separate piece of paper.

When you have gone through all the other systems you have, you need to categorize the list of tasks. Go through and label each task on the list with either an A, B, or C. A tasks are critical, or "Oh my gosh, I can't believe I haven't gotten this done yet. I'm a dead person!" B tasks are important, or "It would be a really good idea if I got this done soon," and C tasks are nice to have, or "It would be nice to do this some-day." Be *very* strict with yourself. Do not confuse "must do" with "would like to do." One client put "organize shoe rack" on her A list. Yes, it is frustrating to spend 30 minutes looking for the mate to a shoe, but it is still not *critical*.

Once you have the complete list and you have identified every task with an A, B, or C, go back to the A's and decide which is *most* critical and put a 1 next to that A, making it A1. Find the second most critical and put a 2 next that A, making it A2, and so on. Do this with all the A's. Now, go to your Air Traffic Controller and decide when you are going to do A1 and write that down.

Most folks can only complete a few A's each day. I recom-mend no more than five A's because A's are frequently more time-consuming or more interactive with others. We don't want you to create a Herculean list for day one, get over-whelmed by not getting it all done, and quit, saying "This is impossible." Have pity on yourself. Remember it is an "Options" list to choose from, not a "Do or Die" list.

**SCHEDULE BIGGER TASKS AS APPOINTMENTS**  As you are assign-ing tasks to specific days, ask yourself how long it will take to complete the task. If it will take longer than one hour, I sug-gest you schedule an appointment with yourself to complete the task. And do not schedule more than six hours of work and appointments for yourself. Surveys have shown that

> If a task will take longer than one hour to complete, sched-ule an appointment with yourself to complete the task.

the average office worker will spend a minimum of two hours each day socializing and/or firefighting.

**REFERENCE OTHER SOURCE MATERIALS** If a task requires other papers, files, or resources, be sure to note that with the task. For example, if you are accustomed to keeping all the papers you need to take action on, on top of the desk, they won't be there now. They will be in, say, the client file. Maybe your own shorthand for client file is "CF." Then write "CF" after the notation of the task to remind you where the supporting paper is.

**MAKE YOUR BEST GUESS** When asked to write down when they are going to do something, many people complain, "I don't know *when* I am going to do some things." It does not matter if your initial guess is correct; the key is to write down the information, giving yourself time to accomplish the task before its deadline. The most important aspect of this exercise is to *write it down somewhere*. The more accurate your guess, the better, but more important is that you simply write it down. You can always move it later.

## 4. ELIMINATE OLD TRACKING SYSTEMS

Once you have transferred all your systems into one Air Traffic Controller, get rid of/stop using those other systems. If it is a joint system (like a family calendar), be sure to let others know they need to notify you if they add anything to the group calendar. And have the courtesy to do the same for them if you change the group calendar. Check the group system at least weekly for updates.

### 5. CREATE A SPECIAL PLACE FOR YOUR BOOK

Create a special place for it on your desk and keep it open at all times. It is hard to make notes in it if it is not open in front of you. It is unlikely you will refer to it if it is not open in front of you. It is difficult to change your daily habits if you keep doing things the same way. Put it open to today in a special place and keep it there, except when you leave the office. When you return, put it back in its special place. There are even fancy tilted pedestals you can buy. Do whatever works for you.

### 6. TAKE AIR TRAFFIC CONTROL WITH YOU EVERYWHERE

When you leave your desk, take your book with you. No, I don't mean if you get up to use the restroom, but I do mean if you are going to a coworker's office to schedule a meeting or a lunch. You *especially* need to have your Air Traffic Controller with you when you go someplace social. Many folks go to lunch with a friend and leave their book at their desks. Stop and think how often a friend says "When can we play tennis?" or "When can we have a couples' dinner?" or "You have to read this book . . ." or "What is Suzie's phone number?" You will use your Air Traffic Controller more in social situations than you realize. Always take it with you.

### 7. TELL EVERYONE WHAT YOU ARE DOING

One of the best ways to become religious about writing everything down is to tell your friends, family members, coworkers, and boss that if they do not see you write down what you just said you would do, they can be assured it will not get done. Now, *they* are committed to you using your Air Traffic Controller! It is always helpful to have others assist you in changing a habit, and it is especially easy when they have a vested interest in your success.

## 8. PERSONALIZE YOUR AIR TRAFFIC CONTROLLER

You will need to embellish on the basic systems detailed here. To start with the calendar aspect is sufficient. As you work with it, you will realize what other sections would be helpful. For example, to remember to take my Air Traffic Controller with me everywhere, I made it my purse by adding a zipper pouch for cash and plastic holders for credit cards and my driver's license. In addition to the calendar system, you may add the following:

- frequently used addresses and phone numbers
- sections for individual projects and organizations
- a plastic zipper pouch for cash
- a few postage stamps in the money pouch for emergencies
- a plastic card pouch for credit cards
- a plastic card pouch for business cards
- a few company brochures
- a calculator

Remember to only carry things you will use every day or at least once a week. Carrying things you use infrequently can add needless bulk and weight.

## 9. ADVANCED AIR TRAFFIC CONTROL TECHNIQUES

First we looked at basic day-to-day use. With a little more planning and effort, we can use other Air Traffic Control techniques to our advantage.

**SCHEDULING BACKWARDS**  We disorganized folks frequently get surprised by deadlines. We believe we have plenty of time to get it all done, then end up scrambling like the proverbial chicken without a head at the last minute. This increases our stress levels as well as the stress levels of those around us, such as office mates, significant others, supervisors, administrative assistants, copy shop employees . . . in fact, everyone we come in contact with gets some of our stress. There is a simple solution: scheduling backwards.

Scheduling backwards works like this. Let's say today is Friday, September 1, and we have to give a report in a month, on Friday, September 30. Planning backwards means asking yourself, "What is the last thing I have to do before actually presenting the report?" The last thing is making the copies and overheads. Therefore, we better make the copies and overheads at least a day in advance, so write that on Thursday, September 29. It will take at least two days to type the report, so write that on Tuesday, September 27. To type the report, we will need to have input from at least three other folks, so we better ask them for what we need at least a week in advance, or Tuesday, September 20. One of those folks tends to procrastinate, so we better remind him on Thursday, the

**Plan backwards to avoid surprise deadlines.**

22nd, that we are waiting. See how that works? Now, rather than screaming at those three folks on September 29, we are asking them nicely on the 20th and giving *them* time to prepare as well.

Since I know *everything* I need to do both for today and from having scheduled important, bigger tasks *backwards*, I can *schedule* time for tasks. I know when I have time to make the phone calls that I need to make. I have maps to the locations I am going to, as well as notes about a conversation to have with the host of my seminar that night.

**IF YOU NEED MORE ROOM FOR NOTES** Be selective about what you write down. Unless you are the designated note taker/secretary for a given meeting, the only thing that requires capturing by you is your tasks and possibly some accompanying details for those tasks. You will get better with time, once you learn to trust Air Traffic Control.

Occasionally, no matter how selective you are, you may run out of room on the notes page. If so, it is easily remedied with either of these two methods. First, you can look back to previous days for a notes page not filled. Write on the bottom of the original page to go to the date of the continued notes. If you fill the second page, look back farther for another blank or not completely used page, note your "go to" at the bottom of the second page, and continue. This is what I do, again, because I am lazy.

If you are more organized, you can carry blank pages in your Air Traffic Controller and insert these as needed. You can add as many pages as you like for a single day. In reality,

> You may want to carry separate blank pages if you record information that may need to come out and be filed someplace else, like in a client's file or a project file.

the need for extra pages seldom arises. Another reason you may want to use separate blank pages is because some information may need to come out and be filed someplace else, like in a client's file or a project file. If you don't have blank pages, or run out and the information still needs to be filed someplace else, just make copies of the notes pages and file the copies. Try to avoid this if possible, because we disorganized abhor extra steps and have difficulty following through. Remember KISS: Keep it simply simple!

## Common Complaints from New Users About Using Air Traffic Control

### "THIS WILL TAKE TOO MUCH TIME"

Some complain that Air Traffic Control will take too much time. Yes, setting it up initially is time-consuming, but

> The notes page replaces the 500 floating pieces of paper, sticky notes, backs of envelopes, and odd scraps with pertinent data on them, reports, agendas, meeting notices, and copies of things you lost once already.

necessary. How long do I spend each day maintaining Air Traffic Control? All told, about 10 minutes, and most of that takes place while talking with someone either in person or on the phone or when I am going through my In Box. I don't make a move without consulting Air Traffic Control first.

## A TYPICAL DAY

Refer back to the sample schedule on page 82. Let's examine this typical day from my personal Air Traffic Controller.

**Today's Options**

There are various things noted on my Today's Options List. They are:

- A note to contact a company that wanted me to do two seminars for them next month. I want to make sure we are still on for this, and need to call the trainer to verify. The original discussion took place eight months ago.

- A note about an interview I need to schedule. I then need to write an article for the organization's newsletter. The assignment was given to me over six months ago.

- A note to get out a specific book to take to a monthly meeting scheduled for tomorrow. I promised someone at the last meeting (approximately one month ago) that I would bring it to her at the next meeting.

- A note to call someone whose name I do not even recognize. Next to it is the date, approximately three weeks ago, to refer back to. When I look back at the referenced date, I will find all the information I need, i.e., phone number, company name, and reason for contacting them.

- A note to call a client that has just gotten back from a two-week cruise. We agreed to schedule an appointment when she returned. The entire time she was on her cruise I did not have to keep calling to see if she was back yet. I knew that I had made a note in Air Traffic Control and the note would come back at the appropriate time for me to act on it. I also got to seem like a really kind, caring person by asking her how her cruise to Jamaica was, not because I remembered, but because I wrote it down to remind myself to ask her! Sh-h-h-h-h-h . . . our little secret.

- A note to begin practicing a speech that I have to give in five days.

- A note to write a client report I have to deliver in two days. I also scheduled time for this in the calendar section.

- An address for someone who called today requesting product information.

- A phone number I was paged from while I was with a client and could not return the call immediately.

- A note to pick up some photos that I was notified are ready today.

Do you begin to see how Air Traffic Control works? Some folks like to segregate their tasks. For example, you could write your phone calls from the bottom up and tasks from the top down (and pray they don't meet in the middle). Or you could write your business tasks from the top down and your personal tasks from the bottom up. There are many variations on how to use this tool. You only need to choose the method that suits you best.

### Places to Go

Next, let's look at the Places to Go section for the same day:

- From 8 to 9:30, I am scheduled to work with a client.

- Between 9:30 and 10:30 I have to deliver a product.

- From 10:30 to 11:30 I am stopping by a friend's house to try to fix her garbage disposal.

- From 12 to 1:30, I am teaching a seminar—the location is written there and the name and contact number of the host.

- From 3 to 4:30 I am working on the report which I have to put in the mail.

- On the way home from the post office I need to drop off a form at a client's home.

I recommend drawing a line from the beginning time to the ending time first, then adding the information, like this. Let's say you have a meeting from 9:30 to noon. First, draw the line. Second, note the information.

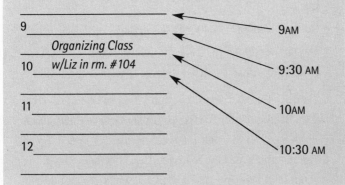

I recommend always writing phone numbers on the appointment if appropriate to facilitate communication. If you get lost or delayed in traffic on your way to an appointment, you can easily locate the number and call. If you need to reschedule an appointment for whatever reason, the phone number is there and saves time over having to look up the number.

You also need to write in *every* appointment you have, no matter how obvious or repetitive. For example, one client was the driver for her son's car pool every third week. It was not written down in her Air Traffic Controller, and sure enough she scheduled something over it three weeks out. Never assume you will automatically remember anything— *always* write every appointment down.

### Notes Page

Finally, let's look at the Notes Page for that same day:

- I have a map to the client's so I can drop off the form.
- The address for someone who requested being on the mailing list.
- Quotes on some carpet I am considering.
- The phone number of someone who called my cell phone when I was driving. I jotted it down to call him back later.

Do you see that all the information I need to operate my day is contained in my Air Traffic Controller? I have notes about clients I need to call that reappear on the day I need to call them, regardless of how long ago the agreement was made to contact them. Air Traffic Control sends me out to my bookcase to get a book for someone for the following day. I am automatically alerted to get out my script and begin practicing my speech so that I will be prepared when the time comes. I can even remind myself to do things I don't understand as long as the details are referenced somewhere else.

People are amazed at how organized I am, and they think I am so very disciplined. In reality, I am lazy. I believe it was Robert Heinlein who said that it is not genius that is the mother of invention, it is laziness. I wholeheartedly agree. The short amount of time it takes me to write things down in a book saves me so much

> You could write your phone calls from the bottom up and tasks from the top down (and pray they don't meet in the middle).

time and stress by avoiding forgotten appointments, unfulfilled promises, and general frustration that I cannot imagine doing it any other way.

### "I DON'T WANT TO DO ALL THAT WRITING"

Guess what? You already are writing most of it down, just not in the same place. You are probably writing most things on sticky notes, desk pads, napkins, matchbooks, torn-off corners of other papers, yellow pads, and the ever-popular backs of envelopes. All I'm asking is that you do what you are already doing, only *all in the same place*.

### "I FORGET TO LOOK IN IT"

Two things about forgetting: First, if you forget to look in your book, you probably have at least one other system working (maybe more) and frequently your tracking methodology is simply remembering things to do and places to go. Second, in order for Air Traffic Control to work for you, you have to have it open on top of your desk at all times, or at least whenever you are there.

### "IT'S TOO HEAVY TO CARRY AROUND"

Some people complain they do not want to have to lug such a heavy book around with them everywhere they go. First, it need not be that heavy, assuming you don't use it as a little traveling filing cabinet. When you pick up your book and hold it upside down by the spine, nothing should fall out. (We conducted this experiment in one class I was teaching and we spent almost five minutes retrieving everything that fell out of just one woman's book!) Staple, tape, or punch holes in anything extra you want in your book that is specific to a given date or event. If it is not specific to an event, there is a good chance you don't really need it. As with your Cockpit, your book should not have anything in it that you use less often than once a week. No "I might need this someday" rat holing.

> An Air Traffic Controller is not that heavy, assuming you don't use it as a little traveling filing cabinet.

### "IT'S TOO HARD TO COORDINATE WITH OTHER PEOPLE'S SCHEDULES"

People often ask me, "But, if I have my own Air Traffic Controller and my spouse has his (her) own Air Traffic Controller, how will we know what the other one is doing?" My suggestion is that . . . well . . . you could try talking to each other. What if you had a special date each morning, over a real breakfast (even if it is not at your home) and discussed your day, or your week, or your plans for the weekend? Communication! What a concept. Like letter writing, it is becoming a lost art. You might even enjoy it.

## For the Skeptic, Ease into It Slowly

I have a simple nonthreatening suggestion. Try it for one month (that is how long it takes to make something a habit). You can endure anything for one month, right? Try it and I guarantee you will become a believer. Those who fight the longest to not use an Air Traffic Controller are the strongest disciples of the tool, once they begin to use it.

> **Try using Air Traffic Control for one month (that is how long it takes to make something a habit).**

## Electronic versus Paper: What's Right for You?

There are many varieties of paper Air Traffic Control systems available, and there are beginning to be many varieties of electronic Air Traffic Controllers, including handheld, laptop, and desktop versions. They have many of the same features as a paper system, or they can be modified to mimic paper systems.

I will be very up-front and tell you I do not recommend the electronic systems—yet. As they currently stand, paper is still quicker, simpler, and more reliable. Studies have shown that it actually requires *more* discipline to maintain an electronic system than it does to maintain a paper system. If you are reading this book, there is a good chance you are disorganized. If you currently have no system, start with paper. If you are successful with paper for at least three months and want to try electronic, then do, but don't get rid of your paper system. Sixty percent of my clients who graduated to electronic have gone back to their old paper systems.

I cannot tell you the number of times clients have complained that the battery for their electronic systems went dead and they lost all their information—appointments, contacts, notes, client data, everything! Another common complaint is that the program somehow got goofed up; when they called the company, they were told the only way to fix it was to reinstall the program. "Will my data be saved?" they query. "No" is the frequent answer. Then they have to try to re-create *everything*, sometimes more than twice before they give up and revert to paper.

Many folks believe that if they cannot manage a paper system, moving to an electronic system will save the day. Unfortunately, that is seldom the case, since electronic systems do require more discipline to maintain.

If you still want to use an electronic system, here are a few recommendations for greater success.

## MANAGE YOUR TASKS

My experience is that folks using electronic systems tend to keep their appointments and their contacts in their systems, but they seldom manage their task lists well. Either to-do's cannot be attached to a particular day, and they wind up with a list of 180 or so tasks to choose from each day, or they simply do

**Tasks are a problem in an electronic system.**

not enter them because it takes too long or is too clumsy. When this happens, they revert to the "I'll leave something out to remind me" method or, even worse, they try to *remember* stuff.

If you are using an electronic system and tasks are an issue, adding a paper system to manage tasks often helps. The paper companion simply needs to be pages, dated one per day, where tasks *only* can be noted. Those old-fashioned desk calendars with two pages for each day and two big rings holding them together can work. They usually have a schedule on one page and blank paper on the other page. Be certain you do not use the schedule page for appointments, even temporarily. Otherwise you wind up with two systems and double the opportunity for errors.

> **If you are using an electronic system and tasks are an issue, adding a paper system to manage tasks often helps.**

Another method is to order the electronic companion from Order from Chaos (see the Resources section). It is the 5.5" × 8.5" format with a place to write tasks and a place to write notes for each day. If you lay your handheld unit on the other page, you still have a single radar screen.

## CARRY A SMALL SPIRAL NOTEBOOK

When you are out of the office, carry with you a small paper spiral notebook (the fit-in-your-pocket size) for capturing tasks. When you return to the office, immediately tear out the pages with the tasks, and enter them into the paper task tracking system. Otherwise, once again, you run the risk of having two systems.

## PRIORITIZING

Attach tasks to specific days. Some electronic systems don't allow you to attach tasks to a given day. They simply live in one master task list. Unfortunately, I do not have a suggestion to solve this, other than going to a paper task list.

Some systems only allow tasks to be given a numerical rank, say 1–10 in importance. All the 1's are grouped, usually in alphabetical order, but you cannot distinguish between 1A and 1B. Printing out the list will allow you to create greater detail. Don't forget at the end of the day to update the electronic list from the paper list to delete completed tasks or add new ones.

Beware of systems where a task is not assigned to a specific day; you must assign an importance to each task when you enter it, even if you will not be completing it for weeks. If you assign a 10 to it, to keep it from bobbing to the top of the list each day until it is due, you run the risk of missing it when it is time because it is at the bottom with the other 10's. This feature requires you to review your entire task list carefully each day.

## KEEP IT TURNED ON

Keep the electronic system tuned to today and your dated task list open on your desk at all times in order to still have a single radar screen for each day. When someone calls for an appointment, check both your calendar *and* your task list to make sure you are not overcommitting yourself. If you

If you use an electronic system, keep it tuned to today and your dated task list open on your desk at all times in order to still have a single radar screen for each day.

have a report you need to write that day and you accept an all-day meeting, you have just overcommitted in a big way!

### IF YOUR ORGANIZATION USES ELECTRONIC

Some organizations require you to keep an electronic calendar for group convenience. If you have a desk job and never leave your desk for meetings or client visits, you should be okay. If, on the other hand, you do have to leave your desk frequently, print out your information for today at the beginning of the day. Attempt to establish a company policy stating that nothing can be added to an individual's schedule 24 hours before the meeting without voice approval. That way at least you cannot get blindsided. If you find you do not have time to work because so many meetings are being scheduled for you, schedule work time for yourself like an appointment as needed.

### FUTURE ELECTRONIC SYSTEMS

Hopefully, some day electronic systems will be better than paper. Reliable voice recognition would be a good improvement. Until then my recommendation is to use paper if possible, and use your electronic system conscientiously.

## Back to Air Traffic Control

There is more about the workings of Air Traffic Control covered in later chapters. For now, just try to get used to writing everything down, writing it all in one place, and writing it in a time-sensitive manner.

## CHECKLIST: AIR TRAFFIC CONTROL

**Rules for Air Traffic Control**
1. Write everything down
2. Write it down in the same place
3. Write it down in a time-sensitive manner so that you have a single radar screen for each day
4. One Life—One System means write everything here, both personal and business, and eliminate all other systems

**How to Create Your Very Own Air Traffic Control:**
1. Acquire/Create an Air Traffic Control System that has
   - Two pages for each day with a place each day for:
     - Appointments
     - Tasks
     - Notes
     - A method for planning months and years into the future
2. Gather together all your current tracking systems which may include:
   - small calendars in your purse or briefcase
   - desk pad calendars
   - wall calendars for vacations, sick leave, conferences
   - company monthly calendars
   - family calendars on the fridge at home
   - information in a computer system
   - paper pads where people take notes at meetings and during phone conversations

- notes or papers in project or client files
- the piles on the desk
- the piles on the floor
- stacking trays with names
- stacking trays without names
- sticky notes
- bulletin boards
- asking someone else to remind you
- things stuck above the sun visor in the car
- notes on the bathroom floor
- e-mails/voice mails requiring action that have not been deleted
- electronic systems (if you have been using one and want to use a paper system instead)

3. Enter everything into your one Air Traffic Control
   - If you are using electronic, consider using a separate paper system for tasks and carrying a small spiral pad when away from the task list
   - If you are using paper:
     - consider capturing tasks on a separate piece of paper first
     - when the list is complete, categorize tasks by ABC 123 method
     - schedule tasks in Air Traffic Control starting with A1 first so as not to overload any one day with too many less critical tasks
   - Schedule bigger tasks like appointments (identified as tasks that will take an hour or longer to complete)

- If you don't know the "when" of a task, make your best guess and go on
- Reference other source materials if needed

4. Eliminate all old tracking systems (including scratch paper, notepads, etc.)

5. Establish a special place for it on your desk and keep it open there whenever you are working

6. Take it with you *everywhere!*

7. Tell your friends and business associates that if they do not see you write something, they should assume it will not get done, so *they* become committed to your change in behavior

8. Personalize your Air Traffic Controller

**Advanced Techniques**

1. Schedule projects backwards

2. Add extra pages/reference previous pages if you need more room for notes

# Step 3:
# The Pending File

This is the shortest step. The Pending File is simply one single file folder, titled "Pending," that lives in your Desktop File and will rapidly become the *most used file* in your office. Its purpose is to hold all odd bits of paper that require some sort of action but are not important enough, or large enough, or ongoing enough to deserve *their own file*. Air Traffic Control got rid of much of the clutter. The Pending File will finish off the rest of it. It works hand in hand with Air Traffic Control to get stuff down on paper, out of your head, and off your desk, until it is needed.

Some of my more creative clients (you know who you are, you right brainers), who like things less rigid and formal, prefer to call their Pending Files "A Safe Place." Then, whenever they need to save something, they put it in "A Safe Place." Whatever you call it, there is one, all-encompassing, unbreakable, cast-in-concrete Pending File Law. That law is:

## NOTHING EVER GOES INTO THE PENDING FILE THAT DOES NOT FIRST GET WRITTEN DOWN IN AIR TRAFFIC CONTROL.

Tasks need to be written down as tasks on the Today's Options list with the supporting paper placed in the Pending File. Appointments need to be written down as appointments on the appointment schedule and the supporting paper placed in the Pending File. Either way, the action MUST be written down first before placing the paper in the Pending File.

*I cannot stress this enough.* To simply put things in the Pending File without first writing them down is the same as throwing them away. They may see the light of day at some later date, when you are rummaging through your Pending File for something else, but it would be an accident, and the Order from Chaos system does not rely on accidents. It relies on planning.

> The purpose of the Pending File is to hold all odd bits of paper that are not important enough, or large enough, or ongoing enough to deserve *their own file.*

The other key to using a Pending File is to put a P with a circle around it *after* the task or appointment in your Air Traffic Controller to remind you where the corresponding piece of paper is.

For example, if you have to fill out an application, but don't want to take the time now to do it, write "fill out application ⓟ" on Today's Options of the day you *will* take the time, with the ⓟ after the task representing the Pending File.

It will take you about a month to automatically remember

you have a Pending File (remember that that's how long it takes to form a new habit). During that first month you may not remember you have a Pending File. When it comes time to fill out the aforementioned application, you could tear your office apart looking for it before you remember, "Oh yeah, that Pending File thing." So to avoid having that exasperating experience, use the circled P to remind you for one month. I continue to use it for items I might not automatically think would be in my Pending File—theater tickets, for example. I put a circled P in my calendar on the day of the event to remind myself what I did with those tickets!

> To avoid forgetting where papers are, put a ⓟ at the end of the task to remind you the paper is in your Pending File for one month.

## How to Set Up a Pending File

1. Create a file folder and write "Pending" on the label.
2. Put it in your Desktop File.
3. Gather all the odd bits floating around the desk.
4. Write down the task or the appointment on the appropriate day in your Air Traffic Controller.
5. Write a ⓟ at the end of the task/appointment to remind you where the paper is.
6. Put the paper in the Pending File and forget about it until you are reminded by your Air Traffic Controller to get it again.

## A TRIP THROUGH A SAMPLE PENDING FILE

Let me just take out my Pending File and peruse it to see what sorts of things are in there.

- An article I need to give to a colleague at a meeting scheduled for next week. (There is a note in my Air Traffic Controller for the day before the meeting to get this article and put it in my "things to take with me tomorrow" box.)
- A letter from a prospective client that I will refer to when I call her (scheduled in Air Traffic Control for tomorrow).
- A list of monthly meeting dates from an organization I belong to that need to be entered into my calendar for the next 12 months (scheduled in Air Traffic Control for next weekend).
- A parking receipt that I need to take to a meeting next month to get reimbursed for (I have a note in my Air Traffic Controller for the day before the meeting to put it in my "things to take with me tomorrow" box).
- Information that came in regarding a seminar I am teaching in two months that I need to review (scheduled in Air Traffic Control for two weeks before the seminar date when I will be preparing).
- Season tickets to the ballet. I ordered them seven months ago and have still not used them all (they live at the very *back* of my Pending File, since they will be used after just about everything else in this file).

The only thing these papers have in common is that they are all represented by a task somewhere in Air Traffic Control. See how it works?

Frequently we disorganized folks have papers representing "unmade decisions" floating around. For example, flyers for professional conferences often come months before we need to attend. When you get one, you are not sure if you will want to go, but what do you do with the flyer until you do decide? Look inside to find the "early bird deadline," you know, where you get a discount. Let's say that is June 1. How long does it take a check request to make it through the chain of command? A week? Two weeks? A month? Assuming it is a month, you will have to decide by May 1 at the latest whether you want to go or not. Go to May 1 in your Air Traffic Controller, write "professional conference? ℗," and put the flyer in the back of your Pending File, because May 1 is a long time off.

When it is time to worry about making the decision about the conference (i.e., May 1), the reminder will jog you to look in your Pending File and make a decision. Meanwhile the conference flyer did not have to live on top of your desk, being shoved from pillar to post, desperately seeking a home or a decision.

Isn't that easy! Now, there should be no extraneous paper on your desk! Not one scrap.

One seminar attendee wrote me and said she thought the Pending File was the best idea she got from my entire presentation. I have noticed that even organized people tend to have a little pile of odds and ends that sit in some obscure corner of their desks. That is their Pending File. The only difference is

———◁══▷———

**Never, NEVER, *NEVER* put *anything* in the Pending File that you do not *first* write down in your Air Traffic Controller.**

————————————

that a physical file called Pending allows you to get those bits scheduled and *off your desk* so you don't have to look at them, worry about them, try to remember them or shuffle through the pile every now and again to see if something is due.

## Electronic Pending File Companion

In the day of e-mail, we are finally getting to the point where some things never reach the paper form but can actually remain as electrons. It is hard to put electrons into a paper Pending File. How do we manage them? By creating a "Pending" folder in your e-mail window. When you come across something you need to take action on later, you first write the task/appointment down on the appropriate day in Air Traffic Control, then drag the e-mail over to your electronic Pending File. It may be helpful to use the P with a square around it to differentiate it from the paper Pending File. We don't want you wasting time needlessly searching the wrong file, now do we?

People have asked me "How often do you go through and clean out your Pending File?" to which I respond, "Haven't you been listening?" If you do this right, the file is constantly being cleaned out as tasks are accomplished and nothing, I repeat *nothing*, should be accumulating.

## CHECKLIST: PENDING FILE

### Rules for the Pending File

1. Before you place anything in the Pending File it must first be noted as a task or appointment in the Air Traffic Control system.

2. Never place anything in the Pending File that is not first written down in your Air Traffic Controller.

3. Write a reminder in your Air Traffic Controller before you put anything into the Pending File.

4. Have I stated it enough times?

### How to Do It

❏ Create a file folder and write "Pending" on the label.

❏ Put it in your Desktop File.

❏ Gather all the odd bits floating around the desk that have no other reasonable home.

❏ Write down the task or the appointment on the appropriate day in your Air Traffic Controller.

❏ Draw a ℗ at the end of the task/appointment to remind you where the paper is.

❏ Put the paper in the Pending File and forget about it until you are reminded by Air Traffic Control to get it again.

## Putting It All Together

At this point you should have accomplished the first three steps in the Order from Chaos method. That means you have mastered the physical environment. There should be no stray scraps of paper, sticky notes, or (especially) piles on your desk. Correct? Before moving on to Step 4 in the next chapter, here is a quick checkup. How do you fare?

> **With the completion of creating the Pending File, you have mastered the physical environment!**

**You have now mastered the physical environment assuming you have done the following:**

- Created a **Vacuum,** having worked backwards beginning at the final repository of oldest stored materials and ending with the top of your desk—tossing, archiving, and labeling as you went
- Created a **Cockpit Office** by
  - placing things you use daily within hand's reach
  - placing things you use weekly within arm's reach
  - placing things you use monthly within the room
  - placing things you use less than monthly outside the room
  - creating a Desktop File with your files currently being worked (touched at least every other day)
  - creating an In Box that is virgin and emptied at least each 24 hours along with all its virtual In Box friends
  - creating a To Read and a To File Box

- Gotten yourself some form of **Air Traffic Control** and
  - written down *all* your tasks on the appropriate day
  - written down *all* your appointments
  - used the notes page for significant daily notes (maps, agendas, minutes, etc.)
  - eliminated all other systems (piles, Post-it notes, computer programs, desk calendars, etc.) and incorporated their contents into the Air Traffic Controller
- Created a **Pending File** for the odd bits and filed them into it, but *only* after having written the corresponding tasks/appointments on the appropriate day in your Air Traffic Control system.

If you haven't completed some of the preceding individual areas, go back and complete them before you proceed! Otherwise, it will be like trying to teach a pig to sing—it will waste your time and annoy the pig.

Assuming you have done all of the preceding, we now proceed to the next stage of completion for the physical environment. Your entire life is not represented solely by your office. Unfortunately, you probably have tentacles of "stuff" in numerous places. Wherever you spend time, you have created stuff: at your office, of course, but also your home, your car, all your disguised luggage, potentially your family members' homes, the gym, and on and on. The only way to have one single system for your life is to *have one single system for your life!* Now, you must gather it all together and deal with it.

## Incorporate Everything into One Single System

### 1. GATHER ALL PAPERS

That means, go forth into your life, find every scrap of paper you have created. Yes, that means the ones behind the tissue box in the bathroom, the ones behind the toaster in the kitchen, the ones over your sun visor in the car, the ones at the bottom of your briefcase or knapsack or purse, the ones under magnets on the front of the fridge—everything, everywhere. It is time to put them into your one all-encompassing system, because each of those other secret stashes represents a system, whether you can verbalize what the system is or not. And the more systems you have, the greater the likelihood you will miss something!

> You should have a single all-encompassing system where everything has a home and nothing gets overlooked.

### 2. MAKE ONE BIG PILE

Pile all those bits and pieces and scraps on your desk in one big stack. (If it keeps falling over or sliding around, you may put it in a box temporarily.)

### 3. FIND EACH PIECE OF PAPER A HOME

Now, stand on your tippy-toes and get the piece of paper on the very tippy-top of the pile and ask, "What is this and where does it go?" Tasks, appointments, and notes get written down in the Air Traffic Controller on the appropriate day. The corresponding paper goes either in the trash, in a file in the Desktop File, in the To File Box to be filed in its home file later, in the To Read Box, or in the Pending File. You will be amazed at how many simply go into the trash.

If you have created a filing system in your home, do the same thing there. Remember to be very clear what lives at home and what lives at the office, and *never* duplicate a file (other than generic ones like To File and To Read). Even a Pending File can be confusing if you have two, so be certain to have a division of labor as to what you do at the office and what you do at home. Otherwise you almost certainly will not have what you need *where* you need it!

When you are done with this exercise you should have a single all-encompassing system where everything has a home and nothing gets overlooked. Now we can personalize it for how *you* work.

## Personalizing Your Cockpit

It is time to look around and design whatever in-basket-type trays, stations, and systems you *personally* need to streamline and simplify *your* office. The simplest way to identify your personal needs is to ask yourself, what tasks do you do repeatedly, and what piles do you make over and over each day? Simplifying and streamlining these daily, repetitive tasks saves tons of time.

### 4. TRAYS FOR YOUR FREQUENTLY CREATED PILES

Those of us who are disorganized are, by nature, pile makers. We can make a pile out of anything. Given enough time, we will eventually be surrounded by our piles. To believe that we will stop this piling behavior is optimistic at best, silly at least. You already have your In/Read/File trays. Since they are stacked, they have a certain "footprint" in your Cockpit. To add other trays on top of (actually in the middle of) these existing trays will not take up any *more* of those precious inches on top of your desk. Therefore, they are a "space" bargain.

> The simplest way to identify your personal needs is to ask yourself, "What tasks do I do repeatedly, and what piles do I make over and over each day?"

**WARNING WARNING WARNING!** Never, never, NEVER have a tray that does *not* have a label on it. If you do, it will simply become a repository of unmade decisions. "I don't know what to do with this . . . so, I'll just put it in this unlabeled tray for now." That unmade decision will live in that tray forever, and it will be joined by all of its "I don't know what to do with this" buddies. It will also make you nervous and increase your stress level because you won't know for sure if those things in the tray are *necessary* tasks just waiting to bite you in the behind. Therefore, *every* tray *must* have a very clear, specific name. "Stuff," "Etc.," and "Miscellaneous" are unacceptable names for a tray! That is just an unmade decision in disguise.

> You may need a tray for your own special interests, such as "Technical Articles," "Websites I Would Like to Visit," "Marketing Ideas," or a tray each for major "Projects."

What other trays might you need? Whatever categories you frequently make a pile out of may be candidates for a permanent stacking tray in your Cockpit.

Remember the rules of the Cockpit as they apply to everything, including your special trays:

- If you use it once a day, it should be in hand's reach.
- If you use it once a week, it should be in arm's reach.
- If you use it once a month, it should be in the office.
- If you use it less often than that, get it out of there.

Do you often assemble a pile of "Things to Take with Me Tomorrow"? I am not a morning person, so assembling what needs to go with me the night before is a necessity. With a "Things to Take with Me Tomorrow" tray I am assured of having everything I need the next day, because I assembled it all the night before, when my brain was still operative. Most office workers need a "Things to Go Home with Me Tonight" spot. Some use briefcases or purses. Whatever it is, make sure it is a predefined, consistent place.

You may need trays for your own special interests, such as "Technical Articles," "Websites I Would Like to Visit," or "Marketing Ideas." Perhaps you need trays for big intensive tasks you perform, such as "Things to Enter into the Computer," "Things to Go to Accounting," "New Claims to Review," or "Stuff to Mail to the Home Office."

Perhaps you need a tray for each major project. One client had five major projects ongoing at the same time. The top of her desk was always covered, layers deep with various bits and pieces from each project, all mixed together! We created five stacking trays, each labeled with the title of one of the major projects. Now, every time something came in for a given project, all she had to do was stuff it in the handy little tray with its name on it. When she needed a piece of information on a given project, she just pulled out the whole pile, thumbed quickly through it (don't forget the 90 percent chance that anything you are looking for is something you filed recently), and that solved that. An accountant had 50 clients, and 50 trays all along one wall of her Cockpit. Unorthodox? Yes, but it worked for her.

Some folks frequently make piles of "To My Assistant" stuff or "To the Boss" stuff. Perhaps you have a coworker you often have things for. Another popular one is a "Signature" tray. Once you know where the things needing signature go, you don't have to leave them on the boss's chair, taped to the phone, tacked to the back of the chair, on the monitor, or any of those other creative places we invent to get other people's attention. When the boss comes in, the things needing signatures are right there, easily found, signed, and placed in their corresponding "To My Assistant" box for redistribution.

Now, ask yourself what other "trays" you need. List them here, then acquire the requisite number of trays, label them, and add them to your beginning In/Read/File tower.

Tray for _____

Tray for _____

Tray for _____

Tray for _____

Tray for _____

One client worked in a building where departments were spread over three floors. Production was on the first floor, Sales (where she was) was on the second, and Accounting was on the third floor. She was constantly making piles behind her on the floor, near the door, for "things for accounting" or "things for production." Unfortunately, she often forgot which pile was which, so she was always reduced to re-sorting both piles before she could deliver them. Also, they had been run over numerous times by the wheels on her chair as she moved around. As you can imagine, their condition was not pristine. We created three hanging trays by her door. The one on top simply had an up arrow on it. The one below that had a sideways arrow on it. The bottom one had a down arrow on it. Now, when she needed to make a pile of things to distribute, they were simply stuffed in their appropriate tray and awaited delivery. How simple (and the accountants were happy because their papers no longer had tire tracks on them—you know how those accountants are).

## 5. STATIONS FOR YOUR FREQUENTLY REPEATED TASKS AND THEIR REQUISITE TOOLS

Let's consider what *stations* you might need to create. Stations represent frequently repeated tasks requiring specific tools. A station includes *all* the tools you need to complete that task without interrupting yourself and without scavenging around for tools. Here is an important point. If you need more than one of a given tool in various locations, get as many as you need. For example, I need a calculator at my computer (to calculate my investments), at my desk (to balance my checkbook), and in my purse (to calculate tax for business transactions). Therefore, I have three calculators, not just one I am always looking for. Most of these tools are relatively inexpensive and if it saves you five minutes a day in interruptions, distractions, and "it was here just a minute ago" moments, you are very soon ahead of the game!

**Stations represent frequently repeated tasks. A station includes all the tools you need to complete that task without interrupting yourself and without scavenging for the necessary tools.**

Let's look at some of the more common stations that many of us need. Remember the rules of the Cockpit:

- If you use it once a day, it should be in hand's reach.
- If you use it once a week, it should be in arm's reach.
- If you use it once a month, it should be in the office.
- If you use it less often than that, get it out of there.

**INCOMING MAIL STATION**  You need a place to deal with incoming mail, both paper and electronic, each day. You may initially place it in your In Box until you have time to deal with it, but eventually you will have to deal with it. Let's imagine you pick up your mail and sit down at your mail station to open it. You will need these tools at least, and perhaps will need more, based on how you work and what you do (remember, you will most likely need an incoming mail station at the office and also one at home):

- *Huge* trashcan, so you can throw most of incoming mail away.
- Air Traffic Controller, so you can write it down and then throw the paper away.
- Hot File so you can immediately file the stuff pertinent to current project/clients and frequently repeated tasks.
- Pending File for the odd bits that have no other home.
- To File Box for archival materials.
- To Read Box for stuff you believe you will eventually get around to reading.
- A *good* letter opener—I prefer the new plastic ones with the razor blade in the elbow. If you are dexterous, the old knife type can work. Either way, don't just sit there and tear the letters open—that will take forever!
- Reading glasses (if you are over 40).
- A pen/pencil to write tasks/appointments/notes with.
- A hole punch to add directions, invitations, agendas, and so on, directly into your Air Traffic Controller.
- Comfortable, spacious, well-lit space to work.

First rule: *Only go through your mail once.* Most of us pick up the mail and immediately start thumbing through it looking for the "good stuff." You know, personal letters, cards, checks—okay, maybe pull out the bills. Once we have cherry-picked it, the rest of the "uninteresting" mail (usually trash if you were honest with yourself) goes on the kitchen counter, or the dining room table, whatever surface is handy, and there it sits. Tomorrow we get the mail, and do the same thing. Now, we have twice as much "uninteresting" mail stacked together. Eventually the counters and tables disappear. Unless, of course, we have company. Then it all gets swept into boxes and bags and stuffed in the closet, the garage, or the "spare" room. We close the door, praying that nobody will open it and see our mess. The boxes and bags sit for days? Weeks? Months? Years? We don't throw them out because we fear something valuable is in there, but we don't have the energy to go through them to find out.

**Rule No. 1: Go through your mail only once.**

*Junk Mail*   The typical contents of the "uninteresting" mail are *unsolicited* junk mail. For example, did the person who is offering you 12 CDs for a penny really send this to *you* personally or could the envelope just as easily have read "occupant"? If you will just throw these things out, *unopened*, you have just eliminated about 75 percent of your mail and virtually all of the bags and boxes behind the closed doors.

We get more mail in a *day* than our parents got in a *week* and than our grandparents got in a *year*. And the volume is growing. Would you say you get more mail now than you got a year ago, or two years ago?

**We get more mail in a *day* than our parents got in a *week* and than our grandparents got in a *year*. And the numbers are growing.**

What about ten years ago? The trend is going up and I don't expect it to reverse any time soon. Face it, paper mail (junk mail), phone mail (solicitors), and e-mail (spam), are *all* out of control. I don't know of a solution other than tossing/screening/deleting everything you did not request without giving it the time of day—*your* precious time in *your* precious day.

*Invitation/Meeting Notice*    So, now that we have eliminated the junk, let's look at the mail that actually deserves some of your time. Say, for example, you open a meeting notice. Go to your Air Traffic Controller, write the meeting information on the appropriate date and *toss the notice*. This has to be one of the most common causes of clutter I've seen—saving things after they have served their usefulness. This is yet another example of our addiction to paper.

*Bills*    Next example, you open a bill. Personally, I do not pay bills until the last possible moment, so I note the due date, back it out one week (if it is due on the 14th I write down "Pay X" on the 7th), and put the bill in my Desktop File labeled "Bills to Pay." What else is in our pile of "good" mail?

*Meeting Minutes/Agendas/Reports*    First, note the date of the next meeting in the Air Traffic Controller. Second, scan the page for any tasks that have been assigned to you and write those in the Air Traffic Controller (planning action ahead of the due date so you have time to complete the task), then *throw the paper away*. You will probably be handed a copy of the last meeting's minutes, agenda, or report at the next meeting.

The number one rule of paper management: If you can get another copy easily if you need it, toss it. What if you toss those minutes, then discover you need a copy later? Whoever wrote them has enough ego invested in their publication that they *always* have an extra copy (nowadays usually on computer) and would be absolutely thrilled to mail, fax, or e-mail (or all three) another copy to you.

*Money*   You receive a check . . . rejoice, do a little dance, and make a deposit slip for it and all its little friends!

*Correspondence*   A personal letter arrives from a dear friend. Savor the moment. Between e-mail and the phone, most of us no longer receive handwritten correspondence. It is a nostalgic treat! Go to your Air Traffic Controller, decide when you have time to respond, be it next weekend, next month, whatever. Write it down, so it does not become one more of those annoying niggling thoughts that keep you awake at night with "Oh darn, I've got to remember to answer Auntie Nancy's letter."

*Newsletters/Brochures/Flyers*   If you have time when you first see these items, scan them for anything of interest to you. If you see anything applicable, note it down, then toss it. If you don't have time to review it now, put it in your To Read Box for later attention. If your scan reveals nothing of interest to you, toss it right now.

*Magazines*    Magazines are always an interesting dilemma. They usually contain things you are interested in. That is why you subscribed in the first place. Unfortunately, most of us seldom have time to read *all* the magazines we receive. Of course, if we don't get around to reading them, we save them, believing we will get around to reading them *later,* when everything slows down. The guilt you feel at not getting around to them is just an added bonus. Here is one possible solution. Figure out how many magazines you actually *do* read in a month; let's say it is three. Pick out your three *favorites,* and cancel the subscriptions to the rest! Our fear is that we might miss something. Well, guess what . . . if you don't read them anyway, you *are* missing it, and your life goes on anyway. We can no longer do everything that is available to us. Accept it and move on.

*Catalogs*    How many catalogs do you receive? Sometimes I receive so many the postal person cannot fit them all in the box! Many I simply toss. My favorites go into a stack where I will have access to them during down time, such as by the television or the bed or on the back of the toilet. The other practice I have is, if I have disposable income at that time, I save my favorite catalogs. If I don't have disposable income at the time, I toss them immediately without even opening them. Why torture myself with things I cannot have?

*Conference/Seminar Notices*    You receive a notice for a professional conference in six months. What do you do? This is a quiz. If you don't know the answer, go back to the Pending File and read it again!

_____
⊂▭▭

**The goal is, after you have opened all your mail, *your desk is clear!***
_____

There are numerous variations on these themes, but this is an average mail delivery for *most folks*. For those items you may receive that were not mentioned, give it a little thought. The goal is, after you have opened all your mail, *your desk is clear!* That is the goal, no exceptions!

*Electronic Mail*    The methodology for e-mail is similar. If it is spam, delete it—you don't have time to read them all. Over 85 percent of the e-mails I get are unrequested. Of the ones you do read, figure out what you need to do. If a quick response is all that is necessary, respond now and move on. If it requires research, conversation with another, or some other time investment from you in order to respond, write it down in your Air Traffic Controller, then either delete the e-mail or drag it over to your electronic Pending File. If it is information, file it in your electronic file system (remember that section in Create a Vacuum) and be done with it.

Treat fax mail the same as normal mail (it is the same only the sender couldn't wait for the U.S. Postal Service).

VOICE MAIL STATION    You may need a voice mail station, too, but this should be quite simple. Do not, I repeat, do not write your messages on a scrap of paper, because that becomes yet another system. Either write when you plan to return the call or perform the requested task directly into the Air Traffic Controller, or, if you get too many every day for that, write them in a specific book, like a yellow pad or a spiral notebook expressly for that purpose. Then go back and rank them with the A (life or death), B (important), C (nice to have) rating. Schedule time in your day to return calls. Then return the A's first, the B's second, and so on. Otherwise, we will make the C calls first, thinking "I'll just get these out of the way," and the next thing you know your time is gone and the *really* important calls are still not made. The danger to an auxiliary system for your phone calls is just that. Sometimes a particular call can be five or six pages back and is in danger of being forgotten. To avoid that dilemma, keep a marker at the place of the oldest unresolved call and move it forward as you elim-inate the old ones. Or just tear off the top right-hand corner of the page when that page is complete. Create some method so old calls do not fall off your radar screen.

> *Do not* write your phone messages on a scrap of paper. Write them either directly into your Air Traffic Con-troller or in a book expressly for phone messages.

OUTGOING MAIL STATION   When it is time to send out any-thing, it needs to be easy. Toward that end, you need an out-going mail station. Assemble and keep handy the following items:

- Assuming you do not have a postage meter, you should have approximately a one-month supply of stamps (including first-class, extra-ounce, oversize, and post-card) in whatever denominations you use frequently.

For example, I send out promotional pens, and the pen, envelope, and one page of stationery weigh just under two ounces, so I have special stamps in exactly the denomination required. Not having to stand in line at the post office every time is a real time-saver.

- A one-month supply of business envelopes.
- A one-month supply of interoffice envelopes.
- A one-month supply of mailing envelopes (whatever size you use most often, 5″ × 7″ or 9″ × 12″, etc.). Many folks recycle used mailing envelopes. This is a good practice, but please, only keep a month's worth, not every one you have ever gotten. Some folks let this practice get *way* out of hand!
- A one-month supply of return mail labels.
- Preprinted mail labels for anyone you frequently mail who does not send preprinted envelopes (some bills are like that).
- Postage scale (nothing fancy).
- Postage charges list from post office.
- Zip code directory, if you use one.

I keep my supplies in one drawer in my desk, the "mail" drawer. When I need to mail *anything*, all I do is open that one drawer and there is everything I need to complete the task.

Here are a few other suggestions for repetitive task stations. Some of us need a bill paying station (which could look similar to the outgoing mail station since many of the supplies are similar), which includes checkbooks, personal return address labels, a calculator, and so on. You may need a Deposit Making Station if the banking function is one of your responsibilities. Or an Accounts Receivable Station, Copying Station, Faxing Station, or a Propaganda Sending Station if you have folks frequently requesting information about your business. Each of these stations may have duplicate tools, like stamps, scissors, forms, or envelopes. If you use certain items in numerous places—have them in *each* of those numerous places.

GROUP STATIONS   If you have an office where the faxing, copying, mailing, and so on, is in a common area, consider setting up fully stocked stations for everyone to use. A group mailing station may include a typewriter, stamps, letterhead stationery, and envelopes, an outgoing mail box, a scale, and so on. Copying stations may need such things as whiteout, tape, scissors, a paper cutter, an X-Acto knife, letterhead, colored paper, pens, and so on. Group stations save *everyone* time, so get everyone's input. It is actually quite fun when tackled as a group.

> If you have an office where the faxing, copying, mailing, and so on, is in a common area, consider setting up fully stocked stations for everyone to use.

Stop and think. What stations do *you* need and what tools should each be stocked with?

Station: _____

Tools:

- 
- 
- 
- 

Station: _____

Tools:

- 
- 
- 
- 

Station: _____

Tools:

- 
- 
- 
- 

Station: _____

Tools:

- 
- 
- 

## 6. REPETITIVE TASKS REQUIRING TRANSPORT OR BOXES

What other things do you have to transport or access often? To avoid wasting time reassembling and re-creating this stuff each time, create boxes for them.

If you belong to an organization and you are responsible for the name tags, you may need a Committee Box. It might contain name tags for the membership, blank name tags for guests, a nice pen for making the guest tags, an organizational directory, blank receipts, and whatever you are asked for frequently. If the tags are pins, you may want to keep some extra tape for those who do not want to make pinholes in silk.

> What other things do you have to transport or access often? To avoid wasting time reassembling and re-creating this stuff each time, create boxes for them.

If you often have to create flyers and such, you may need a Special Papers box. It may include less frequently used supplies, such as transparencies, mailing labels, fancy border paper, gift certificate paper, stickers, and colored papers.

If you are the one who has to set up and staff the company booth when it is used, you may need a Booth Box. Be sure to include such things as screwdrivers (both standard and Phillips), pliers, a hammer, an extension cord, some duct tape, Scotch tape, self-adhesive Velcro, an X-Acto knife or razor blade, pens, paper for making those "back in 10 minutes" signs—you know, all those bits you are always borrowing from the other boothers. Keep a checklist on the top of the box, or inside the lid, of things that cannot live in the box but need to be added each time. This includes current newsletters or current propaganda or current price

> When supplies in the box get low, I make a note in my Air Traffic Controller to get some more. That way I am never unpleasantly surprised.

lists, whatever, so you don't have to reinvent the wheel each time and you will not have to say, "Darn, I forgot the _____."

If you teach classes, you may need a Seminar Box. Mine includes many handouts made far in advance, demo items, blank sign-in sheets, overhead pens and white board pens (in case there are none where I am speaking), brochures, business cards, product lists, extra products, little plastic stands for the things that need stands, and reprints of articles that are appropriate to some students (like a handout on Attention Deficit Disorder). Again, when I have a seminar to teach, I simply grab the box and go, confident that everything I need is in there. When things get low, I make a note in my Air Traffic Controller to get some more. That way I am never unpleasantly surprised. If you teach various seminars, you may need a box for each with, yes, possibly redundant tools in each.

On a more personal note, if you travel frequently, perhaps you should create a permanent travel bag and/or checklist. Since I travel quite a bit, I have a makeup case that is already packed with a duplicate of everything I use, some in miniature, of course. When I am ready to leave, I simply pick up that bag and go—*no packing!* At least not for the toiletries part. I also have a checklist of things I typically pack, such as shoes, jewelry, belts, hose, slips, a nighty; you know, those things that can so easily be overlooked and so disastrous and upsetting to your peace of mind if forgotten. At the bottom of the checklist of "always" items is the "maybe" list, for odd climates or situations, such as "umbrella and galoshes" or "bathing suit and sunscreen" or both. Be sure to take the list with you so if you notice something that you forgot, you can add it to the list and *not* forget it next time. You can't imagine how much time you will save with this little traveling trick. Instead of making packing an ordeal, it becomes a simple matter of following a checklist.

What boxes (repetitive tasks requiring transport) do you need?

Since I travel frequently, I have a makeup case that is ready and packed with a duplicate of everything I use—no packing!

System _____
Contents:

- 
- 
- 
- 
- 

System _____
Contents:

- 
- 
- 
- 
- 

System _____
Contents:

- 
- 
- 
- 
-

System _____

Contents:

- 
- 
- 
- 
- 

## 7. SYSTEM MAINTENANCE

Let's consider some simple maintenance functions required to keep your physical environment organized and running smoothly.

- When individual *files* get too full, cull them right then and there. Do not believe you will come in some Saturday and clean out all your files. You just won't do it. So, instead, when you notice a too full, cumbersome file, just take a couple seconds and get rid of the old stuff. The simplest method is to grab the back half of the paper. If you have been filing chronologically in the front, this *should* be the oldest stuff. Most of this will be old drafts of things, old minutes, old price lists, and just plain old, out-of-date stuff and should therefore be utterly tossable.

> **Do not believe you will come in some Saturday and clean out all your files. You won't!**

- When individual *file drawers* get too full, cull them right then and there, too. Every drawer should have a minimum of two inches of play in it. If it doesn't, it is simply too much work to file. When it reaches the point where we have to wet our fingers and wiggle the paper down into the file, we won't do it. That is when we start the pile on top of the file cabinet saying "I'll file that in just a minute." So, when file drawers get too full, cull them. All you are looking for is an extra two to three inches. You will be amazed, once you start looking, how much you can actually toss. If toss-ing is not an option (e.g., for legal reasons), keep an open banker's box under your desk. When it is full of archivable old stuff, close it, label it in *detail* with what files are in it,

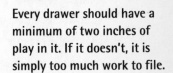

Every drawer should have a minimum of two inches of play in it. If it doesn't, it is simply too much work to file.

and archive it. When you have created that extra two to three inches—STOP! This is not an all-day proj-ect, this is just to get the needed space to file efficiently.

- Keep an eye on your Cockpit. Something you used daily six months ago may no longer be needed. Also, notice when you have to interrupt yourself to get something— maybe your needs have changed. If so, get whatever it is you interrupted yourself for at your earliest convenience and add it to your Cockpit.

- Remember to create and/or eliminate stacking trays, stations, systems, and boxes as needed. The only con-stant in life is change!

## CHECKLIST: PUTTING IT ALL TOGETHER

Before you proceed, you *absolutely must have*
1. created a vacuum,
2. created your Cockpit Office,
3. created an Air Traffic Control system, and
4. created a Pending File.

### Create *One* System for Everything
1. Gather together all the paper scattered throughout your life, both business and personal.
2. Make one big pile on your desk.
3. Find each and every piece of paper a home by either
   - throwing it away because it is now trash (95 percent),
   - writing it down as a task and filing the paper if you need to keep it or tossing it if the written task is sufficient,
   - writing it down as an appointment and filing the paper if you need to keep it or tossing it if the written appointment is sufficient,
   - putting it in the Desktop File if it is a current client or project or frequently repeated task,
   - putting it in the To Read Box if it is reading material,
   - putting it in the To File Box if it is archival material, or
   - putting it in the Pending File if will be acted upon later and has no other home.
   - If you have a Desktop File for your home, do this step in two phases, once at the office and once at home.

**Personalize Your Cockpit**

1. Create other trays for your frequently created piles (refer to previous pages to see what trays you made a note of).

2. Create stations for frequently repeated tasks, including their requisite tools (refer to previous pages to see what stations you made a note of).

3. Create group stations for frequently repeated tasks in common with coworkers.

4. Create boxes for repetitive tasks requiring transport (refer to previous pages to see what boxes you made a note of).


**System Maintenance**

1. When individual files get too cumbersome, check the back half of the papers to see if they can be eliminated.

2. When file drawers get too full to file in easily, cull them immediately to create the requisite two inches of space by tossing or archiving (tossing is preferred).

3. When bookcase shelves get too full to access new materials easily, cull them immediately to create the requisite two inches of space by tossing or archiving (tossing is preferred).

4. Check your Cockpit occasionally to make sure items still meet the daily/weekly/monthly categories and move in or move out tools as needed.

5. Add/delete trays, stations, systems, and boxes as they are needed/become obsolete.

# YOUR FRAME
# OF MIND . . .
# OR INCOMING!

# Step 4:
# Decide <u>NOW</u>!

Got that physical environment under control? Now comes the REALLY hard part—changing your *behavior*. Now, more than ever, it is critical that you spend at least one full week practicing what comes in the next two steps. Let as many people know what you are doing as possible, so they can try to support you in your effort. Remember, when you are under stress you will automatically revert to your old behaviors. All the more reason to ask others to mention if they see you acting inconsistent with your new plan. Be patient. Don't give up. There are some suggestions in this chapter to help you remind yourself and stay on track.

## Typical Behavior

How many times have you picked up a piece of paper, looked at it, said to yourself "I don't know what to do with this," and laid it back down? Later, you pick up that same piece of paper, *still* don't know what to do with it, and lay it back down again. This is both typical and intriguing behavior. What are

**The reason you did not know what to do with all that paper was because you did not have one, all-encompassing system.**

we expecting? That the next time we pick that piece of paper up something will be different? We will suddenly know *exactly* what to do with it? Unfortunately, what to do with it will *not* become more obvious if the paper is allowed to "age." There is no "decision fairy" who will come along and prang you on the head so that the next time you pick up that piece of paper you *will* miraculously know what to do with it! It is plainly and simply an unmade decision.

Prior to reading this book, one of the reasons you did not know what to do with the paper was because you did not have one, all-encompassing system. There was no obvious place for that particular piece of paper to live, so you had to invent a place for it. That process of creating some system for each and every piece of paper is physically and emotionally exhausting. That is where the feelings of depression, exhaustion, and defeat come from. No wonder the piles just kept getting higher. But now you have a system, yes? Now there is a perfectly obvious place for that piece of paper—no decision, no stress, no exhaustion. Unless, of course, it is something you just don't have the time to do but have not *admitted* that you don't have time to do it.

# 1. Gather Real Data

Let's perform an experiment. This is the beginning of week four. You have been engaged in this organizing stuff for at least three weeks and using Air Traffic Control for at least two weeks; therefore, you should have some fairly reliable data.

Look on your task list for the past two weeks. How many of the tasks on your list have you gotten done each day? Include both tasks and appointments. Divide the total number of completed tasks by the number of days you counted and what is that number? Five? Ten? Twenty? Let's say you are Super-Carbon-Unit and you have gotten thirty done each and every day.

> Are you saying "no" 160 times each day or are you saying "no" five or six times and "maybe," "later," and "when I get around to it" 155 times?

# 2. Do the Math

How many pieces of information did we say were coming in to the average businessperson each day? Wasn't that number 190? If you are taking care of 30 each day, that means you are *not* doing the other 160 each day, correct? Therefore, you must be saying "no" 160 times each and every day. Or are you really saying "no" only five or six times and "maybe," "later," and "when I get around to it" 155 times each day?

A big part of "decide now" is figuring out how many times you have to say no every day, then practice saying it. Will this

> **It is absolutely necessary that you spend an entire week focusing on "Decide <u>NOW</u>!"**

make you popular? Will this win you the Miss Congeniality award? The answer is a resounding NO. Especially if you have been the office sweetie with the softest shoulder for crying, the biggest ear for listening sympathetically, or even the biggest mouth for sharing gossip.

## 3. How Many Times Do You Need to Say "No"?

First, how many completed tasks and appointments did you average each day? Subtract that number from 190. That is the number of times you need to be saying no each and every day. Scary, huh?

If you are going to begin to "Decide <u>NOW</u>!" you are going to have to change what you are doing. The definition of insanity is doing the same thing over and over again and expecting different results. Many clients have wanted to get organized and become more efficient and less stressed all while doing exactly what they have been doing all along. "I don't want to change anything I am doing, but I want things to be different." Silly, when you think about it, isn't it? Yet most of us do exactly that somewhere in our lives. Relationships immediately pop to mind, I don't know why . . . ? At any rate, we are all familiar with the behavior, yes? Well, that buck stops here.

## 4. Make and Post Your "No" Sticky Notes

Now do you see why it is absolutely necessary that you spend an entire week (more if you can) focusing on nothing but "Decide <u>NOW</u>!"? Create numerous sticky notes with the words "No 160" (or whatever your number is) written big enough for you to see from across the room. Then stick one of those notes on your phone so when someone calls and asks you to do something you are reminded to ask yourself, "Is this one of my 160 no's?" Stick one note on your computer so when you are reading and answering your e-mail you are reminded to ask, "Is this one of my 160 no's?" Stick one note on your desk pad so when you are opening your mail you are reminded to ask, "Is this one of my 160 no's?" Stick one note on the inside of your Air Traffic Controller so when you are in a meeting with business associates, friends, or family you are reminded to ask yourself, "Is this one of my 160 no's?" Stick them on the door frame in your office so when someone walks into your office and asks you for a favor or tries to pass off one of their no's to you, you are reminded to ask, "Is this one of my 160 no's?"

Don't forget all the other places where you are barraged with requests for your time such as on the cell phone, at the kids' soccer practice, at church on Sunday, at the dinner table at night, everywhere one of those 190 can get to you. Never let down your guard. Be on the alert 24 hours a day, seven days a week, because "they" are. They are seeking *you* out to solve their problems, ease their burdens, fix their mistakes, and generally make them look good.

Does this mean we need to be paranoid? Well, yes and no. Constantly expecting things from you is not something others are doing *intentionally*. It is simply a sign of the times. *They* are as overwhelmed as *you* are, if not more so. They may not possess the secret of knowing exactly how many times they need to say no each day. Therefore, they may be looking for *you* to help them meet all the commitments they unwittingly made that have caused them to be in this overwhelmed state. They are really very nice (harried) people, but dangerous all the same, so *beware*. Also, they can be very persuasive.

## 5. Ask the Magic Question

Now that you are on your guard, let's discuss the practical aspect of this "Decide <u>NOW</u>!" equation. When you first see a piece of paper, 99.9 percent of the time you know everything you will *ever* know about that piece of paper. What most people do not know is *how* to decide what to do with it. So, here are the magic words . . . ready? Ask yourself:

### "What's the task?"

Yep, that's it. It is that easy. All you have to discern from the encounter with that communication is what is expected of you. Many of the 190 pieces of information that come our way each day

> If you don't know *how* to decide, here are the magic words . . . "What's the task?"

are purely informational. We don't have to *do* anything. But we frequently save the paper, message, or e-mail, anyway. NO, NO, NO! It is just more paper. Besides, you can probably get it again if you need it.

## 6. Write It Down

Once you have decided "What's the task?" all you have to do is decide *when* you are going to do it. But you cannot realistically make that decision if you don't have an efficient radar screen for each and every day of your life, now can you? We usually make the decision as to whether we are going to do "it" based on the wrong criteria: "Do I feel like it/not feel like it?" "Do I like them/not like them?" "Will it be easy/quick/fun?" "Do I want them to owe me?" These are *not* valid criteria for this particular decision process, and you know it. But, without an Air Traffic Controller to give you the nitty-gritty about what you have already said you are going to do, you have no other criteria, do you?

Now that you have an Air Traffic Controller, you simply look in it to find a day when you can reasonably expect to be able to do the task and write it down. If there is no room to write it down, then *you can't do it*. Or you will have to delete something else to do the new thing. It is that simple. If it will take you longer than an hour, make sure you schedule it, because an hour will not miraculously appear in your day. Finally, either file the paper in the appropriate place, or put it in your Pending File—if that's where it belongs—and you are done! Now, wasn't that easy? And, you are making realistic decisions, based on realistic data, not just mood and time of month.

Often people say, "But that is not important enough to write down." If it is not important enough to write down, is it important enough to receive any of your precious time? Or is it just another "later" that you are trying to slide by yourself? If it is not important enough to write down, it is not important enough to do!

**If the task is not important enough to write down, is it important enough to receive any of your precious time?**

## 7. It's a Tool—Use It

Conversations with your boss are great opportunities to use this method. When your boss walks in (believing, by the way, that you just sit there with bated breath, waiting for him/her to come in and tell you what to do next) and says, "I want you to do X, right now," you calmly open your Air Traffic Controller, look at the day, and say, "Today I was going to do X and Y and I have these two appointments and then I was going to finish that last assignment you gave me . . . so, which of those things do you want me to *not* do in order to do this new thing?" All of a sudden you are off the hook because *of course* everything you had planned was more important than that harebrained task your boss was suggesting. The Air Traffic Controller is also a great tool in performance reviews because you know exactly what you have done and when you did it. Great record keeping and evidence.

Not knowing *how* to decide what to do with a piece of paper is the first issue. The second issue is for those of you who *don't even try*. Let's go back to that daily mail example. You come home from work. You are tired and it's late. You picked up today's mail and have it in your hand. You thumb through it and pick out the good bits. The rest you just set down on the kitchen counter or table, saying to yourself, "I'll deal with that after I take off my shoes." Yeah, sure! It sits on your counter until you come in the next day, and do it again. How long does it sit there, and how high does the pile get before you deal with it? In the meantime, how do you feel every time you see that pile? Elated? Confident? On top of things? NO!,

> Most piles in our offices and homes result simply from unmade decisions.

of course not. You feel overwhelmed, depressed, out of control. Are these good feelings? NO! So why do we do it to ourselves?

## 8. Stop Believing in Later

We believe in a fairy tale. That fairy tale is "Yes, Virginia, there is a later." Well, guess what . . . there is *not* a later. Not anymore. Perhaps there was 10 years ago or 15 years ago, but not in today's hectic fast lane. You must make these 190 decisions as the information, requests, and messages come at you because . . . **THERE IS NO LATER!**

If you put off deciding, everything simply piles up, and

> We believe in a fairy tale. That fairy tale is "Yes, Virginia, there is a later." Well, guess what . . . there is *not* a later. Not anymore.

you create the same cycle over and over again. Despite what we believe, the mail will not stop being delivered, the phone will not stop ringing, and clients/bosses/friends/family members will not stop asking you to do things. Life will not slow down *later* so you can catch up.

Most piles in our offices and homes result simply from unmade decisions. "I don't know what to do with this" or "I may want to do something about this later" are the two worst reasons to hang on to a piece of paper. If you are not willing to write that task down in your Air Traffic Controller, then how important is it really; is it evidence you are still trying to be all things to all people all the time, including yourself? Often we take on too much, because we do not have one single radar screen for each day. Somebody asks us to do something and *if we feel like it*, we just say yes. Now, you have Air Traffic Control and you can make an educated decision with all the facts in front of you. When do you want to do that, and do you have time? How long is that day's task list already or how full is that day's appointment schedule? If you can't do it that day, can you do it later, or sooner?

## 9. Handle Each Piece of Paper Twice

You have probably heard the old adage "Handle each piece of paper once." I am *not* advocating that. If you believe "handle each piece of paper once," you are letting those pieces of paper decide what you do and when you do it. The first time you see a piece of paper, you most likely have other things that are *more important* to do *at that moment*. Therefore, you cannot realistically handle each piece of paper once, but you should not handle it more than twice: once when you decide what to do with it, the second time when you actually do the task.

## 10. Find a Home for the Paper

If there is not a place for the piece of paper to go, ask yourself "Why not?" You may be thinking too specifically, not in big enough categories. For example, one client has three piles: receipts to enter in bookkeeping system, e-mail addresses to add to contact manager, and updates to the mailing list. We simplified it by creating one file called "Enter in Computer."

Perhaps it really is a new category—that does happen, you know. If that is the case, ask yourself if you need a new file in your hot file or in your file cabinet, or do you need a new stacking tray? New categories do occur, but make sure you are not just being too specific—remember, every file should have at least 20 pieces of paper in it at some point in time, or the title is too narrow.

It is even more important now that you empty every source of incoming information every day, once every 24 hours. That means your In Box, your e-mail account(s), your

> It is even more important now that you empty every source of incoming information every day, once every 24 hours.

faxes, your voice mail(s), your briefcase, your car, anyplace where you put or receive new information/paper. You can't "Decide <u>NOW</u>!" if you haven't even looked!

Remember, spend at least one entire week on perfecting your skills at "Decide <u>NOW</u>!" It is not as simple as it sounds to practice it constantly, consistently, and well. Give it time to become a part of how you think, how you act, and how you do business.

---

### CHECKLIST: DECIDE NOW!

**Assess Your Capacity**

1. Look back into your Air Traffic Controller, count how many tasks you completed each day, and come up with an average.

2. Estimate the number of times you say "no" each day.

3. Subtract the average number of completed tasks from 190 (or whatever you assess your daily average to be) to determine the number of times you must say "no."

4. Create at least five sticky notes with "No!" and the number you arrived at from doing the math above (for example, "No! 170").

5. Post these sticky notes wherever requests for your time come from, such as door frame, phone, In Box, computer, Air Traffic Control, desk pad, dinner table, rear view mirror.

6. Make decisions as requests are made of you.

7. Ask yourself "What's the task?" about everything and everyone.

8. Once you know what the task is, ask yourself "When do I have time to do it?"

9. Find a *realistic* potential date in your Air Traffic Controller and write it down as a task or appointment.

10. When asked to change your plans, use your Air Traffic Controller to illustrate your current plan and request *reasonable* additions or deletions.

11. Stop believing in "later"—there is only "now" and "too late."

12. Handle each piece of paper twice: once when you identify what the task is and write it down as a task or appointment in your Air Traffic Controller, and the second time when you perform the task or keep the appointment.

13. Find a home for each piece of paper. If there does not seem to be a logical place for the paper, ask yourself two questions: Am I thinking about the category too specifically? Is there really a place for it in a larger category?

14. If there is not a place, do you need a new file/tray/ system/station/box? If yes, create it now or make a note in your Air Traffic Controller as to when you will create it.

# Step 5:
# Prioritize Ongoingly

Most of us have made to-do lists before. Sometimes they are for the office, sometimes for home. Now that we have the list, how do we decide what to do first? Frequently we decide to do certain tasks first because they are fun or they are simple or we believe they won't take very long. Sometimes we decide based on what we feel like doing.

Making emotional decisions is the singularly least efficient way to work. How often do you actually finish everything you had planned? Not very often, huh? Given that we won't get it all done, we need to spend our time on the activities that will give us the biggest bang for our time "buck"; those tasks almost never fall into the categories "fun," "simple," "easy," or "quick." How many times have you elected to make a "quick" phone call, believing it will take you three *minutes*, and by the time you are done it actually took you three *hours*?

Often we have worked industriously all day long and been surprised that at the end of the day we still had the really important tasks left undone. Why is that? Frequently the bigger tasks are the *harder* ones, the more *time-consuming* ones, or the *scary* ones—you know, the ones that are outside our comfort zone and require us to do things we are uncomfortable doing. We have also wasted tons of time just rereading the list each time we completed one task and needed to

**Making emotional decisions is the singularly least efficient way to work.**

decide what to do next. Working from an unprioritized list can waste as much as an hour a day, just from rereading the list over and over again.

Most of us have at some point in time (especially when time was tight) graduated to a numbered to-do list. It is common to take a to-do list and, when we realize the list is too long to get everything done today, number the items in order of importance, deciding it is better to get the important things done first. This works better than the "just a list" method, and we save time not rereading the list after each completion.

For those of us who have a problem with procrastination, mastering the "Prioritize Ongoingly" step will help with that, too. Procrastination is an emotional, right-brained experience. When we don't have a daily radar screen, or our to-do list is not prioritized, we ask ourselves, "What do I

**"Prioritize Ongoingly" is actually two separate but related steps.**

feel like doing?" It is an emotional question based on feelings, moods, and attitudes. These emotions have a place, but not in the decision of what to do to be more effective and less stressed. Working from a *prioritized* list, we have made a left-brained, logical decision about what we need to do first. Then, it is simply a matter of looking at the list and finding the 1 and just getting on with it. When you can keep the emotion out of it, you are a long way toward keeping the procrastination out of it, because you are not using another part of your brain. It is not the total perfect solution to eliminating procrastination, but it is certainly a good start. See the following box, which shows different ways to prioritize a list using different criteria.

❑ Buy groceries
❑ Happy Birthday to George
❑ Install new software
❑ Send certificates to participants
❑ Follow up on printing job
❑ Schedule project meeting
❑ Reschedule client meeting
❑ Finish weekly report
❑ Return call to irate client
❑ Research procurement issue
❑ Make copies of research for Steve

What priority did you use? Do you know? Could you verbalize it?

Here is the list again. Let's prioritize it as if our goal is to get a promotion.

1. Finish weekly report (boss sees and may be only information received on my work)

2. Schedule project meeting (need to move project along quick so I'm perceived as a good leader)

3. Follow up on printing job (attention to detail, can't have it wrong with typos or late)

4. Return call to irate client (don't want *this* issue to get elevated to the boss)

5. Research procurement issue (got to keep things flowing smoothly)

6. Reschedule client meeting (boss will never know)

7. Install new software (boss will never know)

8. Make copies of research for Steve (don't want Steve to get ahead)

9. Send certificates to participants (yeah, whenever—it's in the past)

10. Happy Birthday to George (boss doesn't care)

11. Buy groceries (my problem, not the boss's)

Using that same list, what does the prioritization look like if your goal is to improve customer service?

1. Return call to irate client (got to keep the clients happy)

2. Send certificates to participants (best customer is a return customer)

3. Reschedule client meeting (inconvenience the client as little as possible)

4. Research procurement issue (got to make sure customer gets things as quickly as possible)

5. Install new software (better tracking)

6. Follow up on printing job (client won't know so not as important)
7. Schedule project meeting (takes me away from client activities)
8. Make copies of research for Steve (not client related)
9. Finish weekly report (just internal paperwork)
10. Happy Birthday to George (my business)
11. Buy groceries (my business)

I use the criterion "What Will Make Me Money?" Material-istic, you say? It may seem that way, but as an entrepreneur I know if I do not do things that will make money each and every day, I will not be in business tomorrow. You would be amazed at how many entrepreneurs I work with who have nothing on their daily list that will make them money. That is a good way to go out of business fast.

1. Reschedule client meeting (sooner moved, greater odds to schedule appt. in its place)
2. Schedule project meeting (getting paid for this)
3. Happy Birthday to George (ask if he knows anyone who needs my services)
4. Send certificates to participants (ask if they know anyone who needs my services)
5. Return call to irate client (already have the money, just need to fix whatever is broken)
6. Research procurement issue (this will cost money)
7. Follow up on printing job (this will cost money, too)

8. Make copies of research for Steve (this will cost time and money with no obvious return)
9. Install new software (only makes my job easier, so do it on my time)
10. Finish weekly report (internal paperwork—probably won't do at all)
11. Buy groceries (costs money so do on my time)

What happens if your five-year-old son, George, is at home in bed with the flu and it is his birthday? Now how does this list look?

1. Happy Birthday to George (poor little guy)
2. Buy groceries (he needs chicken soup)
3. Return call to irate client (get this out of the way quick)
4. Research procurement issue (solve it ASAP)
5. Reschedule client meeting (just in case I need to be home tomorrow)
6. GO HOME!!! Everything else can wait.
7. ~~Schedule project meeting~~
8. ~~Send certificates to participants~~
9. ~~Follow up on printing job~~
10. ~~Make copies of research for Steve~~
11. ~~Finish weekly report~~
12. ~~Install new software~~

"Prioritize Ongoingly" is actually two different but related steps. "Prioritize" is one step and "Ongoingly" is the other. Let's talk about "Prioritize" first, then we will continue with the "Ongoingly" part.

## 1. Identify Your Priority

**You must first know what *your* priority is before you can decide how to tackle your day.**

For a prioritized list to work you need to first decide what your priority is. What criteria do you use to make that decision?

---

### PRIORITIZING SAMPLES

Here is a generic day's to-do list. At a glance, how would you prioritize it? Use 1, 2, 3 to mark what you would do first, second ... last?

❏ Return call to irate client

❏ Finish weekly report

❏ Research procurement issue

❏ Make copies of research for Steve

---

Stop right here and ask yourself, "What is *my* priority? What criteria should I use to order my day so that when I get to the end I have accomplished the truly important things to forward *my* goals?" If you are an entrepreneur, "What will make me money?" is a pretty good criterion. That way, you do everything that will make you money before you do any of the things that will cost you money. Not a bad plan. And you will be certain to have at least a couple things on there that will make you money because it will be so obvious if you don't.

Your goal may be more personal and not job related. What if your goal is to play the cello in the symphony? Yes, you still need your day job and, yes, you still need to pay the rent. But if your goal is to play cello in the symphony and you haven't touched your cello in five years, maybe something is wrong with this picture.

> **Stop right here and ask yourself, "What is *my* priority?"**

It is not disloyal to have a goal bigger than the job you currently have, and you can pursue something else and still be a good employee. Having another focus does not preclude doing your job to the best of your ability. After all, if the real goal requires money, the better you do your job, the more promotions and/or raises you get, and the faster you reach your other goal—it's win/win.

STOP! What is your priority? Write it here:

_____

_____

_____

## 2. Post Your Priority to Remind Yourself

Take down your "No 160" sticky notes and replace them with the "your priority" notes. You do not necessarily need words.

Pictures can work. For my "Make Money" priority, I just use a "$." For a promotion, you could use just the job title. Get creative. Just be sure you can see one of your priority notes from wherever interruptions are likely to originate.

## 3. Prioritize Your List

Using your same priority, prioritize your list. To do this, you need a system. There are many different ways, just choose a system that works for you.

### MY PRIORITIZING METHOD

The method I use is simple and color coded (many of us disorganized folks are visually oriented and like color). Using a green highlighter (green is my favorite color *and* the color of money), I first read down my list, looking for the tasks that will make me money. When I find one, I highlight the space in front of it. When I get to the bottom, I go back and say "Which green item will make me the *most* money," and I put a 1 in that green square. Next, I ask which green item will make me the second most money and I put a 2 in that green square, and so on. Once that is done, if there are more moneymaking tasks than I can do between 8 and 5 (business hours), I use a purple highlighter to mark tasks that I can do *after* business hours. Last (and unmarked) on my list are the things that are free or will cost me money. I make sure I do *everything* I can to *make* money before I do *anything* that will *cost* me money.

## THE ABC 123 METHOD

First go through your list and rank each task with one of these three letters:

- A = Life or Death tasks—if I do not do this today something will die, perhaps an opportunity, perhaps a relationship, but something will die.
- B = Important—it is important that I get this done today, but not life or death.
- C = Nice to Have—it would be nice to get this done today.

When you have assigned each task a letter, go back and look at all the A's. Which A is *most* important? Put a 1 next to that A, so it becomes A1. Then decide what is the second most important A. It becomes A2, and so on. Do this with the B's and C's as well. Now, start to work with A1, then proceed to A2, all the way through C10, or whatever.

### THE RIGHT METHOD FOR YOU

You can use any variation of these methods. Perhaps instead of ABC you use color. Your favorite color is pink so A's become pink. You are ambivalent about green, so B's become green. You *hate* orange, so C's become orange. Or one color is business and another is personal, or one is during business hours and another is after business hours . . . whatever works for you! It doesn't matter what method you use, as long as you use *some* method. Otherwise you are back to procrastination, basing decisions on feelings, and wasting time rereading the list.

## 4. Prioritize Ongoingly

Now that you have identified your priority and prioritized your list in your Air Traffic Controller, it is time to address the "ongoingly" part.

What we don't realize is that most of us who create a prioritized list let it end there. As soon as we get a phone call, someone walks into our office, or we just see something lying on top of our desk, we might as well throw the list out the window, because we forget all about what we decided was the most important thing to do today and let other people decide our priority for us. The danger with that method is that everyone believes *they* are the center of the universe and their problem is *the* most important issue facing the nation at that moment. Certainly, they have *our* best interests at heart and would *never* waste a moment of our precious time. Right? The truth is that the only person who will *truly* have *your* best interests at heart is *you!* Letting others decide for you is seldom in your best interest, and whatever issue they approach you with was almost certainly not on your list of things to do that day.

But we, as human beings, are preprogrammed to respond to someone else's emergency. Perhaps it is in our lizard brain along with fear of fire and fear of heights. Whatever the reason, we confuse "urgent" with "important." Does that mean that if it is urgent that it is *not* important? Certainly not, but the converse is even less true. You need to examine the importance, not respond to the urgency.

Be aware that we have created a business culture where we are all expected to be interruptible. You are considered rude, self-important, or antisocial if you close your door or don't answer your phone every time it rings. If you work in a cubicle, you don't even have a door. So, now that we are *totally* interruptible, here is a little statistic about those interruptions: 85 percent of them are a complete waste of your time; only 15 percent are worthy of

> As human beings, we are preprogrammed to respond to someone else's emergency. We confuse "urgent" with "important."

your attention. Yet most of us respond to any interruption, whether it is an 85 percent or a 15 percent. And you wonder where your day goes?

## 5. Measure Each Interruption Against Your Priority

If 85 percent of the interruptions waste your time, how do you identify the 15 percent to pay attention to? You measure everything that comes at you against *your* priority. For me the question is "Will this make me money?" If the answer is no, I get rid of the interruption. If the answer is yes, I deal with it. Now

> Are you giving your coworkers and friends positive reinforcement for interrupting you?

do you see why it is so important to *know* what *your* priority is? If you don't know your priority, you have no ruler to measure against.

## 6. Measure Each Item That Matches Your Priority Against Your Present List

You measure *all* items that are consistent with your priority against the progress you have made on your already prioritized list. For example, if you have reached a task "buy groceries" and someone comes in and says she has a problem with a memo she is writing, helping her is probably *more* important (unless you are a caterer). If, on the other hand, you are on "soothe irate client," helping the new person with her memo is more likely to be *less* important. To use this powerful "urgency meter," you must KNOW YOUR PRIORITY and HAVE A PRIORITIZED DAILY LIST in your Air Traffic Controller *and* you must LOOK AT IT. Put in terms of the single radar screen, you need to know which plane needs to land first to meet schedule, not let any old plane land first just because it asked nicely or hysterically.

## 7. Stop Encouraging Bad Behavior in Others

Are you giving your coworkers and friends positive reinforcement for interrupting you? If you stop and listen, no matter how trivial the issue is, or go with them to their office to help them with their computer glitches, or if you are the one who stops by for a chat just because you were nearby, you are encouraging the 85 percent of interruptions you don't want. Therefore it will be even harder for you to get them to stop,

A client of mine who is a minister orders her day based on the question "Will This Get Someone into Heaven?" I'm not certain how ministers would make that decision, but then we assume they must teach them about it in divinity school. That is how she prioritizes first her list, and then her *day*. Every visitor, every phone call, every e-mail is scrutinized using the same criterion, "Will This Get Someone into Heaven?" If not, she simply says, "I'm on a deadline right now. Could you come back at 4 P.M.?" Interestingly, most non-heaven-related visitors understand and go away, *and* few ever return at the suggested time. They were usually passing time or just wanted someone to listen to them whine (remember they *are* the center of the universe, just ask *them*).

and worse, get them to stop expecting you to act the way you always have. It's like a dysfunctional family—they are going to try to drag you back into your old behavior. Expect them to use guerrilla tactics like crying, snubbing you, whispering behind your back, ceasing the conversation whenever you walk into the room, and glaring at you. Expect this and more. If you stick to your guns, only responding to the 15 percent, eventually others will come to *expect* your new behavior. Then they will enforce it even when you don't. But be patient. Behavioral changes don't happen over night, for you or for them.

## 8. Fill in the Heart Line

I maintain I can predict where anybody will be in 10 years, just by looking at their to-do lists in their Air Traffic Controller. How, you ask? If your list has only "taking care of business," "what I have to do to survive" items on it, I predict that in 10 years you will still be right where you are today, doing exactly what you are doing, and still wishing things were different. What makes it to our to-do lists are "treading water" tasks. Yes, they will keep you at your job, possibly even get you promotions and raises, but they are very shortsighted—using a microscope to direct your life, not a telescope.

If, on the other hand, your list has things bigger than you, such as charitable activities, or items that are oriented toward larger goals and visions, then I predict you will accomplish your goals and be doing something different and wonderful 10 years from now. Often, we see our goals as something far in the future—too far away to take action on now or too big for little ol' me to ever accomplish. But, as some famous person said, if not now, when? If not you, who? Some of us expect our goals to somehow miraculously accomplish themselves at some distant point in the future. If you want the scenery to change for you, consider putting at least one thing on your list every day that is a step toward a larger goal, something that is not just treading water.

**If not now, when? If not you, who?**

There are many methods for goals setting available. My experience has been that the sheer complexity of most of those methods precludes our following through with them.

Most are hard to implement and even harder to maintain, and they eventually fall by the wayside in our busy, complex lives. The beauty of the Order from Chaos system is that it is simple, and you can work on as many goals at the same time as you want. If you are making one baby step toward one of ten concurrent goals, eventually you will accomplish them all.

In the Order from Chaos Air Traffic Controller (see the Resources section), the top line on each day's list has a heart next to it. This is where I write one thing each day that will take me one *baby step* closer to a larger goal. If you do not use one of my planners, take your favorite color highlighter and color in the top line on your to-do list for each day. Do not write anything on that line until that day when you are prioritizing your list, and then make sure it is a baby step toward a bigger goal.

No, I don't mean putting on your list "write great American novel." It is too big to accomplish in a day. If the task is too big, we are daunted by the sheer scope and will not take any action. The criterion for deciding on the task size to write is, can you accomplish it and check it off at the end of the day? If the answer is yes, then it is small enough to be included. If the answer is no, then it is too big, will daunt you, and therefore will remain uncompleted.

The second reason to break goals down into baby steps is because to accomplish anything worthwhile, you first need to do your homework. Instead of "write great American novel" put "locate evening adult fiction writing class" or whatever you see as

> **To accomplish anything worthwhile, you first need to do your homework.**

the first step. You don't even have to enroll. Just locate one. Then, tomorrow, write "enroll in adult fiction writing class" or whatever the next baby step toward your goal would be. Remember, it has to be small enough to check off at the end of the day. If you take one baby step each and every day, you *will* get there. (How do you think *this* book got written? One tiny step at a time, and here it is. I think it took about four years, from conception to publication, but I did it using exactly the method I am describing to you here!)

Remember our cello player from earlier in this chapter? She had a dream to play with the local symphony *and* she had not touched her cello in five years. She began to write on her heart line things like, get cello out of closet, locate sheet music, service bow, tune cello. Pretty darn basic, huh? But each day she did one little thing—some tasks took less than 30 seconds—and she checked it off at the end of the day. Eventually her tasks progressed to "practice 30 minutes" and "advertise cello lessons" and "schedule symphony audition dates." Last I heard she was not yet with the symphony, but I have hope that she will be by the time this book is published.

The added benefit to her employer is that, as a person, she is happier. And happy employees make better employees and create a more pleasant working environment. Even though her vision is not work related, her employer still benefits.

My goal is a personal crusade. I believe we have created such a user-hostile business environment that it is killing us all. We *need* less stress in our jobs. At the same time, we are doing more with fewer workers due to layoffs, attrition, and scarcity of qualified candidates; therefore, we need to be more productive. I believe my six-step method can increase productivity while decreasing stress for all of us. My goal is that the GNP of the United States will go up 5 percent and it will be my fault, because we are all too productive and unstressed (read happy!). How's that for grandiose? And I am working toward that one baby step at a time, each and every day.

If we do *not* make daily tiny progress toward our most cherished goals, most of us will just stay in survival mode, and in survival mode the scenery never changes. Survival mode means making the same New Year's resolution year after year, seeing the same images, and sighing and saying to yourself "someday. . . ." Stop dreaming about it and finally do something about it. Climb your symbolic Mt. Everest, and do it one baby step at a time.

> **If we do *not* make daily tiny progress toward our most cherished goals, we will just stay in survival mode where the scenery never changes.**

## The Corporate Version

This step may seem small in the scheme of things but imagine an entire company where every employee is using the Order from Chaos six-step method. They are all working from a prioritized list and sticking to that prioritization all day. All the president of the company would have to do is say, "Prioritize based on customer service," and, ZAP, the entire company is focused on customer service. Or the president says, "Prioritize based on the bottom line," and, ZAP again, the entire company shifts focus. Employees frequently have the best of intentions, but management does not communicate what the focus needs to be. Add to that the fact that we are all very distractible and we have created and embraced a business culture of expected interruptibility. No wonder companies frequently don't accomplish what they set out to do. Now you can begin to see how the Order from Chaos six-step method can change business practices in America. What a powerful tool!

### CHECKLIST: PRIORITIZE ONGOINGLY

1. Identify *your* priority.
2. Create sticky notes (to replace the "no" stickies from last week) with your priority, or a symbol of your priority, and post them in all the places where requests for your time come from: door frame, phone, In Box, computer, Air Traffic Control, desk pad, dinner table.
3. Choose a prioritizing method.
   - Favorite color method.
   - ABC 123 method.
   - Invent your own method.
4. Prioritize your list each day using your priority.
5. Fill in the heart line on today's list:
   - Make it a baby step—small enough to be checked off at the end of the day.

- Progress toward a larger goal or vision.
- Make it something that is bigger than you—like a charitable activity.
- Make it something that makes your heart sing.

6. Prioritize each and every interruption, new piece of information, and request for your time against *your* priority.

7. If it matches your priority, measure it against your progress on your prioritized daily list.

8. Stop giving "the squeaky wheel" positive reinforcement for negative behavior—discourage and eliminate the 85 percent of the interruptions each day that waste your time.

9. Review with your boss, or yourself if you are the boss, the potential benefits to an entire company using this method!

# Step 6:
# Daily Habits

Here we are at Step 6, Daily Habits. You should have completed all the previous steps, yes? Now, what are you going to do *every day* to maintain the delightful order you have created in your universe? Unfortunately, organized is not a depot where you arrive; it is a state of mind you must live in.

No matter how perfect your Cockpit, how complete your Air Traffic Controller, how orderly your Pending File, how adamant you are at Deciding <u>NOW</u>! and Prioritizing Ongoingly, you still need to perform daily maintenance to keep your kingdom orderly. The good news is that it should not require more than 10 or 15 minutes of dedicated time each day to maintain your system. Some of that time will be spent planning your day, some ending your day, and some cleaning off your desk. But, it must be done, *religiously*, each day or chaos will return, and return quickly. It doesn't take long for 190 pieces of information each day to take over again. Once the chaos is back, you are back into overwhelm and the piles win. So gird your loins and read on.

**You need to perform daily maintenance to keep your kingdom orderly.**

## Plan Your Day

### 1. PRIORITIZE YOUR LIST

Everybody has a plan for their workday. For some of us it is to put on a hard hat and a bulletproof vest and pray we get to the end of the day with a minimal amount of blood loss. That is a plan, but there is a better one. Assuming you have done Steps 1 through 5, you now have your daily radar screen in Air Traffic Control with your prioritized task list. You must do this *before* your day starts; otherwise you will never get back to it, no matter how good your intentions.

Say, for example, a typical day for you starts by coming in the front door, only to be attacked by fellow workers and their crises. By the time you actually get to your desk you already have managed three emergencies and taken on seven more. You hit the ground running and plan to find a quiet moment later to plan your day. It won't happen. What you will do is go from emergency to crisis to brush fire all day. If this is your typical day, then consider planning in the car in the parking lot at work, *before* you enter the building. If while attempting this coworkers begin attaching themselves to your windows like giant suckerfish, then perhaps you need to plan sitting in the driveway at home before you drive to the office. If family members do the suckerfish routine, maybe you need to consider stopping at a park between home and work and planning your day there. It doesn't matter where you plan, only that you do it *before* the feeding frenzy starts, or you will never do it (then we are back to the hard hat and bulletproof vest scenario).

## 2. REVIEW YOUR APPOINTMENTS

Planning your day includes first prioritizing your list, but second is reviewing your appointments. When review-ing your appointments, check to make sure you have all relevant reports, copies, references, files, notes, lists, numbers, and maps. Check for things you promised to bring to someone, such as arti-cles, books, and information or phone numbers. Remember, you should have assembled it all in one place (the "things to take with me tomorrow" box, or the "going outside the office" box) and already have everything you need with you.

> **When reviewing your appointments, check to make sure you have all relevant reports, copies, references, files, notes, lists, numbers, and maps.**

Make certain you have whatever you need to ensure each appointment is the best use of everyone's time. How often have you sat in a meeting with someone who was not pre-pared? Pretty much a waste of time, huh? So don't *you* be the one who wastes other people's time. Be prepared, and you can assure that you will be prepared by planning your day, every single day.

Even if you realize as you are planning your day at 8 A.M. that you do not have X report for the 3 P.M. meeting, you *do* have seven hours to prepare it. Or you can call the attendees and reschedule. (Of course, you *should* have scheduled the writing of the report in your Air Traffic Controller well in advance so as to not get caught like that, but, oh well, everything takes practice. At least you will learn from your mistake and not do it again, right?) But, the bigger point is, you will be prepared, not caught off guard.

## 3. SCHEDULE LARGER TASKS AS APPOINTMENTS

The third thing to do while planning your day is to look at the items on your list and, based on priority, decide which ones need scheduled time. I have to schedule time to make and return phone calls, since I am seldom in my office between 8 and 5. I schedule a minimum of three hours of phone time each week, wherever a natural hole at the beginning of the day occurs, and then I forward all phone tasks to that day. Also, I honor that prescheduled phone time. If I have to schedule something else there, I must *first* find someplace to reschedule that phone time.

## 4. FILL IN THE HEART LINE

Finally, while planning your day fill in the heart line. Make sure you have at least one task or appointment each day that moves you toward a bigger goal, or else the scenery will never change.

When should you plan your day? It may depend on your personal schedule—when you are at your best. I am not a morning person. Never have been. For me to prioritize my day first thing in the morning would be a disaster, not to men-

> When should you plan your day? It may depend on your personal schedule—when you are at your best. If you are a morning person, don't even consider planning your day the night before.

tion how long it would take me. Therefore, I plan my day the evening before. No matter how late it is, I am at my best in the evening (from 10 P.M. to 2 A.M., in fact); therefore, I take advantage of my personal best time. If you are a morning person, don't even consider planning your day the night before. You are probably tired, dull, and not in the least interested. Take advantage of when you are at your best because this is a *very* important step.

## YOUR GREATEST ALLY

We have discussed how to prioritize your list. Does that guarantee that this is exactly how your day will go? Of course not! We will be interrupted, driven off course, distracted, sidetracked, diverted, and otherwise confused. But what it has done is get our greatest ally on our side—our subconscious. You will be amazed how different things can be if you just tell your subconscious "This is what I want today to be like."

A good example of the power of the subconscious was

> You will be amazed how different things can be if you just tell your subconscious "This is what I want today to be like."

when my book agent was trying to find a publisher for this book. She called me early one morning and said, "You need to have at least 10 national speaking engagements on your calendar before we send your manuscript to publishers." "No problem," I said, while writing "10 nat'l spkg engmts" on my heart line for that day (notice my personal shorthand method). There I sat, looking at "10 nat'l spkg engmts" and saying to myself, "How the heck do I do that?" By the end of the day, I had received two phone calls from national organizations. One wanted me to speak at five events they had planned across the country. The second wanted me to speak at three events they had planned. After the second call, I called my book agent back and said, "I have eight national speaking engagements. Is that close enough?"

Would those two agencies have called me that day anyway? Maybe. Would I have accepted? Probably not, because they were going to cost me money to do. But because "10 nat'l spkg engmts" was on my list, things were different. It is like magic. I can't explain it. I don't need to explain it. I just know it works, and I just do it. With my greatest ally, my subconscious, doing whatever it does to make the universe fall in line with my desires, life is simply easier (and more mysterious). Besides, who would want to live in a universe that they could explain, anyway?

## 5. SCHEDULE FOCUS TIME AS NEEDED

There is a phenomenon that occurs in the human brain that we'll call "flow." You've experienced it. It is when every cell in your body is focused on the task at hand; time stands still; you forget to eat; you forget to go to the bathroom; there are not insurmountable problems, only solutions you have not yet thought of; and the end product is way better than your usual work. Recognize this description? Can you remember a time when this happened to you? That is flow. It takes the average human 20 minutes to get into flow. It also takes a nanosecond to get out of it, if we are distracted by a ringing phone, a barking dog, a coworker sticking their head in just to say hi! We think we go right back into it, but, in reality, it takes another 20 minutes to achieve the same state of flow. Given that, how productive is it to constantly shift from one task to another and back again, just because some new shiny object caught your eye?

**When organizing entire offices, I frequently recommend scheduling regular uninterruptible hours.**

Much of the work we do can be interrupted with no dire consequences. You can check your e-mail, sort through your In Box, or make copies while being interrupted and the end result will be basically the same. Then there are those tasks that require us to focus, concentrate, and get into flow. A task that would take you one hour to complete when you are not interrupted will take an average of four hours if you are. No wonder we never get anything done!

If you have to do focused work, close your door and lock it with a "don't even think about knocking" sign on it, turn off your phone, close the blinds, turn off the "you've got mail" bell. Eliminate *all* possible distractions before you begin to work. Remember, it will save you three hours for every hour of work. If barricading yourself in is not an option, consider working someplace else. Perhaps you could schedule yourself into a conference room for the duration. Maybe working at home is an option. Go to a library, the basement, or an empty gymnasium—whatever it takes to not be bugged by interruptions.

When organizing entire offices, I frequently recommend scheduling regular uninterruptible hours. You could take calls and walk-ins between 8 A.M. and 9 A.M., between 11 A.M. and 12 P.M., between 1 P.M. and 2 P.M., and between 4 P.M. and 5 P.M. You could work on more difficult work between 9 A.M. and 11 A.M., and 2 P.M. and 4 P.M. Another possibility is that you and a coworker who have somewhat interchangeable roles take each other's calls on rotation. If you are the morning person, you work on focus work between 8 A.M. and noon, then take calls for both of you in the afternoons. Your counterpart (hopefully a night person) could take calls for both of you in the morning and do project work in the afternoons.

Perhaps you arrange to work at home one day a week, say every Wednesday or Friday (Fridays are usually slow anyway, aren't they?). Could you arrange to work at home two mornings a week, coming in at 11 A.M.? Maybe leave early, at 2 P.M. on Monday, Wednesday, and Friday. There are as many possibilities as there are willing participants. Maybe half the office tries it and the other half doesn't, then compares notes in two weeks. Nothing ventured, nothing gained.

The caveat here is you must work. Sometimes working at home is even *more* distracting than at the office, especially if you have small children at home or if you yourself have trouble focusing. If you do decide to work at home some hours, you will have to create your Cockpit there as well, or you are back where you started.

### 6. ONE TASK AT A TIME

So now that you know where you are going to work, how are you going to work? The work method I recommend is to first assemble whatever files and supplies needed for Task 1 on your list. Make sure only those things needed for that task are on your desk. Otherwise you run the risk of distraction. Focus everything on Task 1 until it is complete. Put away the files and supplies from Task 1. Assemble files/supplies needed for Task 2, and so on.

> First assemble whatever files and supplies needed for Task 1. Focus everything on Task 1 until it is complete. Put away the files and supplies from Task 1. Assemble files/supplies needed for Task 2.

### 7. WORK YOUR PLAN

Remember, as new activities come in, measure them against your busy radar screen and your prioritization method to help decide whether to say "Yes, come in" or "No, go away."

Will planning your day ensure that that is the way it will play out? Of course not! Nothing can guarantee that anymore, not with cell phones, e-mail, faxes, and open door policies. But having a plan and working that plan does increase the odds that you will get to the other side with a greater feeling of accomplishment, knowing you spent your time wisely and efficiently and accomplished as much as humanly possible in these hectic times.

> Having a plan increases the odds that at the end of your day you will know you accomplished as much as humanly possible.

## End Your Day

One of the qualities we have lost as our lives have sped up is *closure*. We don't stop working because we are done anymore, although some of us can remember a time when we did. Times have changed. Now we stop because we are out of time. Last I heard, the average workweek is up to 47.5 hours, up 1.5 hours from a couple years ago, and growing. We always leave with tasks undone, information unreviewed, and piles unsorted. Even when we are not on the job, our brains are still thinking about what we just did, or what we need to do next.

> Last I heard, the average workweek is up to 47.5 hours, and growing. We always leave with tasks undone, information unreviewed, and piles unsorted.

### 8. SAVE FIVE MINUTES BEFORE YOU LEAVE

We need closure, endings, the opportunity to say "I am done!" That is the purpose of ending your day and the gift it will give you. Think of it as planning your day, only backwards. Save five minutes at the end of the day, before you rush out to your next appointment or home to fix dinner. Open up your Air Traffic Controller to your radar screen for today and look at your list. Take a moment . . . how did you do? Remember to stop and give yourself credit for what you *did* accomplish!

What if you only accomplished seven things today? If they were the seven most important things you

> If you accomplished the seven most important things you had to do today, you are among the 3 percent of human beings on the face of the earth who did.

### A TYPICAL ENDING

We rush out of the office thinking about what we left undone and what we need to do about it tomorrow. We may even stuff some papers into a briefcase, planning to carve a few precious moments out of our hectic personal lives to try to catch up at home that night. As we are driving we are wondering and worrying how we are going to get that report done, or that review, or return all those phone calls. Are we conscientious, courteous, defensive drivers? Hell no! We are dangerous, angry, preoccupied maniacs on the road.

When we finally get home to our family and friends, we are not fully present to them because we are still thinking "Now tomorrow I need to..." When little Suzie comes up with her latest masterpiece, we glance distractedly down and respond in our automated voice, "That's nice, darling," and return immediately to our private world of worry. Trying to sleep at night is probably the worst. We lay awake worrying about all the unfinished tasks, including the ones stuffed in the briefcase lying in the living room whispering to us in urgent tones. We wake up at 3 A.M. with the "Oh no, I forgot to ____ (fill in the blank)!" When we finally wake up the next morning to the shrill of the alarm (how long has *that* been ringing?), we are still as exhausted as when we went to bed because WE NEVER STOPPED WORKING!

had to do today, you are one of the elite 3 percent of human beings on the face of the earth who accomplished the seven most important things they have to do each day. It is an exclusive club (and a successful one as well).

To end your day, every item should have some mark next to it. To keep it simple, you only have three options. Those three options are a check mark for done, an arrow for rescheduled, and an X for no longer an issue. Let's look at each in a bit more detail.

## 9. CHECK OFF ALL COMPLETED TASKS

A check mark (✔) says this task is done, finished, complete. Your goal is to get as many check marks as possible. Science has discovered that putting a check mark next to a completed activity releases endorphins in your brain, so if you need a little pick-me-up, complete something and check it off!

Did you ever get to the end of the day, look at your list, realize you didn't do anything on the list, so you write down what you did do just so you can check it off? Now you know why—you wanted those endorphins!

## 10. RESCHEDULE ALL UNCOMPLETED TASKS

An arrow (←) means you did not get that task done today, but it still needs to be done, so you must reschedule it somewhere in the future. There are two caveats about rescheduling. The first is *move tasks consciously*, not automatically. For example, don't

**Move tasks consciously, not automatically.**

just move a task to tomorrow. Look at your whole radar screen for future days, both tasks and appointments, and decide when you can *realistically* expect to complete this task.

The second caveat is *never, never,* **NEVER** *make the arrow, then write the task in the future*. ALWAYS rewrite the task, *then* go back and make the arrow. Otherwise tasks can fall between the cracks. For example, you put an arrow next to the "call irate client" task and as you are about to find a future date to write it, the phone rings. It is your best friend who wants to go out to dinner next week. You start thumbing through your Air Traffic Controller to find a good night and write it down. The conversation ends. You go back to ending today. You see the arrow next to "call irate client." You think it has been moved (because you *did* go through the motions) and you move on. That task has just been dropped, and you will not know that it has been dropped until the client calls you, or the order cancellation is received, but certainly *not* at the right time.

If you have tried this before and your complaint is "All I ever do is rewrite stuff," then you probably have one of two problems. One, you are not prioritizing *ongoingly*. If you make a list, then don't work it and let the 85 percent of the interruptions that waste your time eat up your day, then of course you will have to rewrite. Two, you may be being a bit overzealous and optimistic about what you can accomplish in one day. If your list runs off the page each day, you are probably overcommitting. Remember when we talked about looking back to see how many things you have gotten done historically and adjusting your expectations to be that number? How many check marks do you average per day? Five? Seven? Ten? Now, limit yourself to that many tasks on a day. Try that for a week or so and consider it an exercise in reality.

Also, over time you will develop your own shorthand. If you have to make a call to a person and have the phone number and a few notes about a conversation on June 7, then have to move it forward to June 10, just write the person's first name with a question mark after it and put 6/7 after the question mark. When you get to that task, you will realize you are asking yourself "Did Janie call me back?" If the answer is yes, you get a free endorphin-producing check mark. If she didn't call you, then just turn back in your Air Traffic Controller to the 7th and there are all your notes and her phone number and everything you needed to know. Plus you hardly had to rewrite anything. Feel free to be creative, as you come up with your own shorthand tricks. Remember, no information in your book is ever lost, unlike the scribbles on the backs of envelopes, but you may have to search around to find it.

## 11. ELIMINATE ALL UNNECESSARY TASKS

An **X** means "remove it from my list!" Sometimes we write down something, especially when we are writing far into the future, that, by the time we get there, may have become a moot point. In that case, cross it off and move on. Or you thought doing something was a good idea, but now that you look at it, you decide not. Cross it off and move on.

Here is a little trick that, if you will use it, will keep you from turning into Sisyphus. If you have moved a task forward

> If you have moved a task forward *five times,* you are facing a 97 percent chance that you will *never* do it.

*five times,* you are facing a 97 percent chance that you will *never* do it. It will be because of one of these reasons:

1. It is way *outside your comfort zone,* and you are avoiding doing it. You need to do it. It is imperative that you do it, but it is just too scary. If this is the case, make it Task 1 tomorrow and *just do it.* Tell someone you are going to do it and ask them to check with you and see if you did it. If you *still* don't do it, mark it off and get out of it regardless of the importance.

Getting out of things is not as hard as we believe, sometimes. Make the phone call and say, "I'm sorry. I know I said I would do X but my schedule is unfortunately busier than I thought it would be and I simply cannot do this. Dan has the requisite skills to do this. You may want to give him a call. His number is 123-4567. I still want to help, so don't take me off your list. Keep me in mind for future activities. Bye." Fun? No. Necessary sometimes? Yes. Remember, people mind changes less than they mind surprises. So don't wait to the last moment to renege. Give them time to find a replacement. Admittedly this is not possible with every task, but at least consider the possibility.

2. The task has no deadline or nobody harassing you to do it, so you are just not getting around to it. Ask yourself why you are not doing it and how important it really is. If it is truly important, consider rescheduling it to when

there is a bit of pressure for a deadline. Not *last* minute, but more pressure than "sometime in the next three months." Reschedule it one last time as Task 1. If you don't do it then, mark it off and get out of it.

3. It is something you feel you *should* do. We all occasionally take on things out of guilt, peer pressure, or a desire to look good. We offer to do a favor for a friend, then realize we don't really have time. We schedule exercise when we really *hate* exercise but feel like we should exercise. These are not very motivating reasons to do anything. Your mother is not here, and you don't have time for "shoulds." You only have time for the "musts" and "need tos." Mark that *should* off and move on!

> Your mother is not here, and you don't have time for "shoulds." You only have time for the "musts" and "need tos." Mark that *should* off and move on!

## 12. CROSS THROUGH THE ENTIRE DAY

Finally, after every task on today's radar screen in my Air Traffic Controller has some mark next to it, I add an extra *huge* endorphin rush and draw a big dark line through the whole day! If you had a blood pressure cuff on me at that moment you would see my blood pressure plummet, because I just gave my brain permission to stop thinking. Does that mean I don't still have to do all those things that are written in the future days, weeks, and months? Of course not. But it does mean that I have done as much

> Ending my day means I can SHUT OFF MY BRAIN!

as is humanly possible for today. That is the moment when I run a hot bubble bath, get a good old-fashioned English murder mystery and a glass of red wine, and RELAX. I have *closure* with my day and I am *done*. I can SHUT OFF MY BRAIN!

Being a night person, I also move the page marker to tomorrow and glance at tomorrow to be sure I will not be blindsided by something. Believe me, if for some reason I do not end my day, I continue to worry, "Have I missed anything important? Is there something that is going to 'get' me tomorrow?" It is not a pretty sight. Even if I get a migraine and am about to take pills and lie down, I still take the extra few minutes to end my day. Believe me, the medicine works much faster when I am truly and honestly relaxed.

Now, when you leave the office with your day ended, you have a relaxed saunter in your step. You notice how utterly gorgeous those flowers blooming by the car are. You drive home, relaxed, courteous, letting other drivers in just to be nice (why is she scowling like that?, you wonder). When you get home and little Suzie comes up with her newest drawing, you say, "What a lovely pink horse." "It's an elephant!" she replies. "Well, why don't we go draw some pink horses then?" At dinner you ask your family members how their day went and you actually have the energy to listen to their answers. At bedtime, you lie down, with an angelic little smile on your face and drift effortlessly off to sleep. You sleep soundly through the night and wake up relaxed, refreshed, and looking forward to the new day. What a difference—all because you ended your day and gave your brain permission to shut down.

## Clean Off Your Desk at the End of the Day

One last thing is to clean off your desk at the end of the day. The best analogy I can think of is a dinner party. Have you ever had a dinner party when you were too tired (or too tipsy) to clean up afterward and you said to yourself, "I'll do it tomorrow"? And do you remember how you felt the next morning, coming out to confront last night's mess? Somehow, during the night the crud fairies visited and made it much much worse, didn't they? You can't start anything else until you have cleaned up that mess. Kind of puts a damper on the whole day, doesn't it? You are doing the same thing to yourself each time you come into a messy desk. It is yesterday's crisis, yesterday's messes, yesterday's issues. As with the dinner party mess, you cannot start today until you clean up yesterday. As soon as you start that, you get sucked into some morass of yesterday quicksand and your elegant plan for today is derailed once again. So don't go there!

> Cleaning up your desk at the end of the day should take no more than five minutes.

Cleaning up your desk at the end of the day should take no more than five minutes—especially if you have a **Cockpit Office** where everything has a home, and an **Air Traffic Controller** where you can write it all down, eliminating the need to leave anything out to remind you anymore. You have a **Pending File** where you can put the odd bits that have no other home. You have been making **Deciding <u>NOW</u>**! as things came at you all day and **Prioritizing Ongoingly** those decisions. You **Planned Your Day,** worked that plan, and **Ended Your Day.** Cleaning off your desk at the end of *that* day should be a snap.

On the other hand, if you haven't been using the Order from Chaos six-step method, how much paper can pile up in a week, a month, a year, a lifetime? Some of you know the answer to this firsthand, don't you? Remember, cleaning off your desk includes cleaning out/off/up every carrier you use daily, that is, your In Box, your e-mail, your fax machine, your voice mail, your briefcase, your backpack, your purse, your passenger seat, your llama, your whatever!

Now, drive home, enjoy the gorgeous sunset, be present with your family and friends, fall easily asleep, dream sweet dreams, and awake refreshed and renewed.

## CHECKLIST: DAILY HABITS

Each and every day, religiously for no more than 10 to 15 minutes, perform these three activities to keep yourself simply on track!

### Plan Your Day
1. *Before* your day starts, prioritize your list.
2. Review your appointments.
3. Schedule larger tasks as appointments (scheduling no more than six hours of appointments or task work).
4. Fill in your heart line.

5. Acknowledge that you have enlisted the help of your greatest ally—your subconscious.

6. Schedule focus time as needed and arrange for location.

**Work Your Plan!**

1. Assemble tools for Task 1.

2. Begin work on Task 1.

3. When you are done, put away everything from Task 1.

4. Assemble tools for Task 2.

5. Begin work on Task 2.

6. Continue in a like manner until the day is over, saving the last five minutes to perform end-of-the-day tasks.

**End Your Day**

1. Review your day.

2. Give yourself credit for what you *have* accomplished.

3. Check off each completed item (receiving your mandatory endorphin rush).

4. Identify tasks to be rescheduled later and

   • first, identify when you can reasonably expect to complete the task.

   • rewrite it, using your own personal shorthand to make the rewriting as simple as possible.

   • return to today's list and draw the arrow in front of the forwarded task.

5. Eliminate all unnecessary tasks. If the task has been forwarded five times, do whatever you can to eliminate the task from your list *forever*.

6. Cross through the entire day.

**Clean Off Your Desk at the End of the Day**

1. Any papers or tools left on your desk at this point should be
   - placed in their appropriate spot in your Cockpit.
   - written down in your Air Traffic Controller.
   - placed in the Pending File, if appropriate.
   - Include your briefcase, backpack, purse, passenger seat of your car, your llama . . .
2. Do not leave any piles anywhere or they will haunt you!

Finally, shut off your brain and enjoy your life! You are ORGANIZED, and you know how to stay that way!

# I'M DONE . . .
# SO NOW WHAT?

# I'm Done . . .
# So NOW What?

That's it! Sound doable? As a fellow disorganized person, I have attempted to design a system for us that is simple, easy to use, and easy to maintain. It is no frills, down and dirty, cut to the chase. Yes, it may take a bit of time to set up, but once you rid yourself of a lifetime of detritus, maintenance is a few minutes a day. That is why it is one week at a time, one step at a time. Trust me, it *is* the best way to do it.

Yes, I said a few minutes a day. Don't think you can blow it off all week and think you will be able to catch up on the weekend, or Friday afternoon or Monday morning before you start. You must be *committed* to do a few minutes each day or, no matter how good your

> Don't think you can blow the plan off all week and catch up on the weekend, or Friday afternoon or Monday morning.

intentions, YOU WILL NEVER DO IT, and you will find yourself right back in the middle of the chaos of your own making. Bite the bullet and JUST DO IT.

A quick review of your one, complete, all-encompassing system that accommodates your 190 pieces of information each day plus anything and everything else:

- You have a **Cockpit Office** where the tools you use most frequently are handy and you know where things go and everything has a home.
- You have a single radar screen for each day in **Air Traffic Control,** where you can write everything down so you can get it out of your head and off of the desk, bulletin board, monitor, and sun visor.
- The odd bits now have a safe home in the **Pending File** and will be there when needed.
- All day you **Decide <u>NOW!</u>,** making informed decisions as things come up, asking "What's the task?"
- You are **Prioritizing Ongoingly** with each piece of paper, each phone call, each visitor, because you know what *your* priority is and you follow it through to the end.
- You **Plan Your Day** before it starts and enter each day prepared and focused.
- You **End Your Day** and get closure so your brain can rest and you can enjoy your life.
- You **Clean Off Your Desk at the End of the Day** (including all virtual "desks") preparing the way for tomorrow.

**Now do you see why I say this six-step method will increase your productivity and decrease your stress?**

Now do you see why I say this six-step method will increase your productivity and decrease your stress? Last are a few things to do to keep it all working.

# Regular Maintenance

- Review the tools in your Cockpit occasionally to be certain you have not stopped using some as frequently or started using others more frequently.
- Check your hot file weekly. Are those files still hot? You will probably add at least one and remove at least one each week (yes, things change that quickly; we only *think* they don't).
- Clean out your Air Traffic Controller so it doesn't become a little traveling filing cabinet. Apply the Cockpit rule to it; that is, do you use everything in there daily, or at least weekly? If not, do you need it?
- Order a new one each year before you need it (like in October) so you have it when you need it.
- Go through your Pending File every couple months to make sure any deleted items' paperwork has not been left behind.

- Check monthly to see if you still have the right stacking trays and stations and boxes. Do you need new ones? Are the old ones still being used frequently enough?

- Are you still Deciding <u>NOW</u>!? Are you saying "no" enough? If you fall back, put your sticky notes back up— retrain and reinforce! Remember, Decide and Prioritize are the two behavioral steps that will be the hardest to make part of your daily behavior.

- Are you still Prioritizing and doing it Ongoingly? Again, if not, put those sticky notes back up.

- Constantly improve your own shorthand for Planning and Ending your days. The less time you spend writing, the more time you have for your life!

- When a file is too full and starts to bug you, take 30 seconds and clean it out. If you have been filing chronologically in the front, just grab the back half and see what can be tossed (you'll be surprised).

- When a file drawer is too full, take a quick gander at it and see what files can be tossed or at least archived. Keeping an ongoing banker's box in the closet for archives makes it quick and simple. Remember, it has to be easier to be organized than it is to be disorganized or we won't do it.

Remember, the only constant in the universe is change, especially if the policies and procedures manual is to be followed!

# Support Systems

In the beginning of this book I recommended you do this process with at least one other person, a friend, a coworker, your entire office, whomever. One of the reasons for that suggestion is that once you are done, you will still need some sort of support to keep you on track. Remember, we are talking about changing a lifetime of bad habits.

If you did this process with one other person, schedule regular checkups with each other. A monthly lunch works well. Review the six steps and talk about what is working and what is not working. Sharing ideas on personal discoveries and issues often helps the other as well.

If you did this process with your whole office, spend at least five minutes at a monthly staff meeting discussing it. Perhaps each month one person could talk for five minutes on one of the steps, whichever step they felt most accomplished in or had experienced the greatest improvement in. Maybe you turn it around and it is the person who needs help in a certain step and the rest can support them with ideas and help. Get creative! Make a game out of it. Give awards for the most impressive Cockpit or the lightest Air Traffic Controller, or maybe to the person who is the best at Deciding <u>NOW</u>! or the person with the greatest improvement in productivity or the greatest reduction in stress—visible and emotional signs allowed.

> **Give awards for the most impressive Cockpit or the lightest Air Traffic Controller, or maybe to the person who is the best at Deciding <u>NOW</u>!**

You could start a group in your area. Put a sign up at the bookstore where you got this book with your phone number and a request for others interested in continuing the discussions. Perhaps the bookstore themselves would be willing to coordinate a group (never hurts to get people into your store, whatever the premise). You could put up your sign at an office supply store. Check at your office, if you read this alone, for interested parties, or at your church, or at your PTA. With 60 percent of businesspeople suffering, it should be relatively easy to find other sufferers in your area. And misery loves company. If nothing else, it is always reassuring to find out you are not the only one who loses stuff and misses appointments.

You could even start a group online. If you have an interest in this, contact me at liz@orderfromchaos.com and we can set something up at my website.

One of the best ways to really learn the six steps is to teach them. If you share an office with someone, teach them what you know, how you think the area should be set up and run, and agree on how you will work together. If you and your life partner share a desk at home, set it up using this technology; then teach him or her what you have done so he or she can share in it (and not mess up *your* system!). Whatever you do, do something! Otherwise, this will be just another book you read and forget.

# If You Fall Off
# the Wagon . . .

One student took the class over a year ago. He was quite gung-ho during the class and for quite a while after as well. Slowly, one little bit at a time he said to himself, "I don't need to do/maintain that part. It will still work." Eventually, piece by piece, the entire system fell away. One day he almost missed three (moneymaking) appointments. Suddenly he realized he was back to no system at all, just where he had been before he took my class. Amazingly (to him, not to me), he was able to go right back into the full system almost immediately and is one of my most dedicated disciples to this day.

What do you do if you fall off the wagon? Get right back on. Once you have the system set up, reinstating it is relatively simple. The detritus that has accumulated may take a while to sort through, but you know how to do it, you know about Cockpits, Air Traffic Controllers, Pending Files, Labeled Stacking Trays,

**What do you do if you fall off the wagon? Get right back on.**

Stations, and Systems. Much of that should still be in place. With a little updating it should work for you again. Then all you have to do is begin again to Decide <u>NOW</u>!, Prioritize Ongoingly, and begin your daily habits of Planning, Ending, and Cleaning.

# Resources:
# What If I Want More?

Once you have read this book, there are many forms of reinforcement available from Order from Chaos. You can get a one-hour audiotape or CD with a quick overview of the six-step methodology. Play it whenever you need a boost (it is pretty funny and entertaining as well as informative).

You can get the entire six steps, one entire tape on each step in order to focus on one area, or just those to reinforce what you are already doing. This format is available on CD as well. We have mouse pads with the six steps to keep in front of you and screen savers with animated little steps. We also have Air Traffic Controllers that you can order. By the time this book is published, I'm sure we'll have more. Check the website at orderfromchaos.com for the latest and greatest (and prices).

That's it. If you have any questions, comments, recommendations, praise, testimonials, anything at all, please feel free to contact me. My contact numbers are:

Voice: (505) 345-1153
Fax: (505) 341-9525
E-mail: liz@orderfromchaos.com
Website: www.orderfromchaos.com
Address: Liz Davenport
Order from Chaos
1305 Van Cleave NW
Albuquerque, NM 87107

now . . .
Go GET Organized
and STAY Organized